mentor Lernhilfe

Englisch

7./8. Klasse

Grammatik und Wortschatz: Teil 1

Astrid Stannat
Dieter D'Zenit
Willi Mey †

Mit ausführlichem Lösungsteil

In Zusammenarbeit mit Langenscheidt

mentor
Eine Klasse besser.

Die Autoren:

Astrid Stannat, Studienrätin für Englisch
Dieter D'Zenit, Fachlehrer für Englisch (Hauptschule), Referent in der Lehrerfortbildung
Willy Mey †, Schulamtsdirektor, Referent in der Lehrerfortbildung

Illustrationen:
Christiane Hansen, Hamburg,
Susanne Becker, Jutta Bauer, Hamburg

Layout:
Sabine Nasko, München

© 2005 mentor Verlag GmbH, München

Das Werk und seine Teile sind urheberrechtlich geschützt. Jede Verwertung in anderen als den gesetzlich zugelassenen Fällen bedarf deshalb der vorherigen schriftlichen Einwilligung des Verlages.

Umwelthinweis: Gedruckt auf chlorfrei gebleichtem Papier.

Der Text dieses Bandes entspricht der seit 1.8.2006 verbindlichen neuen deutschen Rechtschreibung.

Satz: Franzis print & media GmbH, München

Printed in Germany
ISBN 978-3-580-65545-7
www.mentor.de

Inhalt

Vorwort 5
Benutzerhinweise 6

A *Die Zeitformen des Verbs* 7
    Test 15
    Word power: Wörter lernen mit Bildern 18

B *Englisch reden? – Kein Problem!* 20
    1. Jemanden kennenlernen 20
    2. Fragen stellen: Welche Fragetypen gibt es? 27
    3. Seine Meinung äußern 32
    Test 36
    Word power: Nachschlagen im Wörterbuch I 37

C *Die Verwendung von past tense und present perfect* 39
    1. Simple past und present perfect 40
    2. Simple past und past progressive 48
    3. Der Gebrauch des present perfect mit *since* und *for* 50
    Test 55
    Word power: Hören und Sprechen 57

D *Can, must, may – und ihre Ersatzformen* 59
    1. Das unvollständige Hilfsverb *can* 59
    2. Das unvollständige Hilfsverb *may* 62
    3. Das unvollständige Hilfsverb *must* 64
    4. Die unvollständigen Hilfsverben *can, must, may*
       und die Zukunft 70
    Test 72
    Word power: Nie wieder sprachlos! 74

E *Die indirekte Rede* 76
    1. Die Zeitenfolge in der indirekten Rede 78
    2. Weitere Veränderungen in der indirekten Rede 82
    3. Fragen in der indirekten Rede 84
    4. Befehlssätze in der indirekten Rede 88
    Test 91
    Word power: Nachschlagen im Wörterbuch II 94

F *Some – any, much – many: Unbestimmte Pronomen* 96
    1. *some – any* 96
    2. *each – every* 99
    3. *much – many – a lot (of)* 100
    4. *(a) little – (a) few* 101
    Test 102
    Word power: Lesen 104

G Das Passiv 106
    1. Die Zeitformen des Passivs 107
    2. Aktiv und Passiv 111
    3. Das Passiv in Verbindung mit *can, must* und *may* 114
    4. Das persönliche Passiv 116
    Test 118
    Word power: Rechtschreibung 120

H Der Genitiv 122
    1. Der *s*-Genitiv 122
    2. Der *of*-Genitiv 126
    3. Der Genitiv ohne nachfolgendes Substantiv 127
    4. Der „doppelte" Genitiv 129
    Test 131

Lösungsteil 133

Register 157

Vorwort

Dear friend,

Dies ist ein Buch, das nicht in der üblichen Weise – nämlich von vorne nach hinten – durchgearbeitet werden will. Du kannst selbst am besten entscheiden, welcher Stoff dir Schwierigkeiten bereitet und daher vorrangig geübt werden sollte.

Einige Hinweise zum Aufbau des Buches sollen dir helfen, dich zurechtzufinden:

Die Hauptkapitel beschäftigen sich jeweils mit einem bestimmten Aspekt aus den Bereichen Grammatik, Wortschatz und Sprechfertigkeit. Nachdem du dir ein Kapitel herausgesucht hast, solltest du dieses Kapitel auch ganz durcharbeiten. Auf eine kurze Einleitung folgen Regeln, Beispiele, Übersichten und jede Menge Exercises und Games, die aufeinander aufbauen und daher nicht übersprungen werden sollten.

Am Ende jedes Kapitels kannst du anhand eines Tests deine Kenntnisse überprüfen. Die Testauswertung findest du gleich im Anschluss. Trage die Anzahl deiner richtigen (und falschen) Lösungen in dein Personal scoreboard ein und lies die entsprechende Bemerkung, die zu deiner Punktzahl passt.

Mit der richtigen Lerntechnik fällt dir vieles bedeutend leichter!

Deshalb findest du auf den Word power-Seiten, die wir zwischen den Hauptkapiteln eingeschoben haben, jede Menge Lerntipps zum Thema Wortschatz. Lass dich überraschen!

Wir hoffen, dass dir die Arbeit mit diesem mentor-Band Spaß macht und dir Erfolg bringt.

Autoren und Verlag

Benutzerhinweise

 Das hier ist Fred. Er wird dir in diesem Buch noch oft begegnen. Fred möchte dir beim Englischlernen mit Rat und Tat zur Seite stehen.

 Hier findest du eine wichtige Grammatikregel.

 Hier erfährst du Wichtiges über Grammatik und Wortschatz.

 Exercise: Dies ist entweder eine Aufwärmübung am Anfang eines Kapitels oder eine Übung, in der du das bisher Gelernte anwenden sollst.

 Game: Durch Spiele wollen wir dich anregen, frei Englisch zu sprechen.

 *Test:* Hier kannst du überprüfen, ob du alles verstanden hast und auch richtig anwenden kannst.

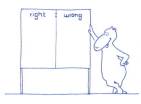 *My personal scoreboard:* Hier kannst du dein Testergebnis eintragen.

A
Die Zeitformen des Verbs
The tense forms

A camping holiday

Um auszudrücken, dass sich etwas in der Vergangenheit ereignet hat, für die Gegenwart zutrifft oder sich in der Zukunft abspielen wird, hast du die Auswahl unter zahlreichen verschiedenen Verbformen. Aber wer die Wahl hat, hat manchmal auch die Qual! Hier hast du die einmalige Gelegenheit, dir einen Überblick über die am häufigsten verwendeten Zeiten *(tenses)* zu verschaffen.

Schau dir den folgenden Zeitstrahl an – er soll dir helfen, die verschiedenen Zeiten einzuordnen:

Vergangenheit		Gegenwart		Zukunft
past perfect	*simple past*	*present perfect*	*simple present*	*future*
Tim had eaten	*I ate*	*I have eaten*	*we eat*	*I will eat*

Das **present perfect** steht zwischen Vergangenheit und Gegenwart, weil es beide Aspekte in sich trägt. – Damit beschäftigen wir uns später noch ausführlicher.

Zeitformen des Verbs

Zunächst wollen wir uns aber genauer ansehen, **wie** die verschiedenen Zeiten **gebildet werden**.

Zu jedem unregelmäßigen Verb findest du im Wörterbuch 3 Formen. Die erste Verbform ist der Infinitiv *(infinitive)*, die 2. Form ist die Form der Vergangenheit *(past tense)* und die 3. Form ist das Partizip Perfekt *(past participle)*. Diese 3. Form brauchst du, um das *present perfect* und das *past perfect* zu bilden.
Bei den regelmäßigen Verben stehen die 2. und die 3. Form nicht dabei, weil sie immer gleich gebildet werden.

> **Regel**
> Bei den regelmäßigen Verbformen wird in der 2. und 3. Form einfach *-ed* angehängt.

1. Form (infinitive)	2. Form (past tense)	3. Form (past participle)
(to) stay	stayed	stayed
(to) call	called	called
(to) move	moved	moved
(to) clean	cleaned	cleaned

Endet ein Verb im Infinitiv auf **Konsonant + y,** dann wird in der 2. und 3. Form *-ied* aus der Endung:

(to) empty	emptied	emptied

Endet ein Verb auf einem stummen *-e*, dann wird nur noch ein *-d* angehängt:

(to) move	moved	moved

Nach einem kurzen Vokal wird der auslautende Konsonant verdoppelt:

(to) stop	stopped	stopped

> Bei den unregelmäßigen Verben ist es etwas komplizierter – am besten prägst du dir gleich alle drei Formen des jeweiligen Verbs ein; dann hast du bei der Bildung der Zeiten keine Probleme:

(to) eat	ate	eaten
(to) see	saw	seen
(to) go	went	gone
(to) begin	began	begun
(to) throw	threw	thrown

Zeitformen des Verbs

 In der folgenden Übung sind die Regeln für die Bildung der verschiedenen Zeiten aufgeführt. Trage die richtige Bezeichnung für die jeweilige Zeit ein:

simple past
regelmäßige Verben:
-ed an die Grundform

unregelmäßige Verben:
2. Form

futur I
will + Grundform des Verbs
im Mündlichen: *'ll* + Grundform

simple present
Grundform des Verbs
3. Pers. Singular *(he, she, it)*:
-s wird angehängt

past perfect
had + 3. Form
(-ed oder unregelmäßige Form)

present perfekt
I, you, we, they   *have* + 3. Form
he, she, it   *has* + 3. Form

Zeitformen des Verbs

  Hier kannst du zeigen, wie fit du im Hinblick auf unregelmäßige Verben bist!
Zeichne die fehlenden Luftballonschnüre, sodass jeweils alle drei Formen eines Verbs bei Fred zusammenlaufen.

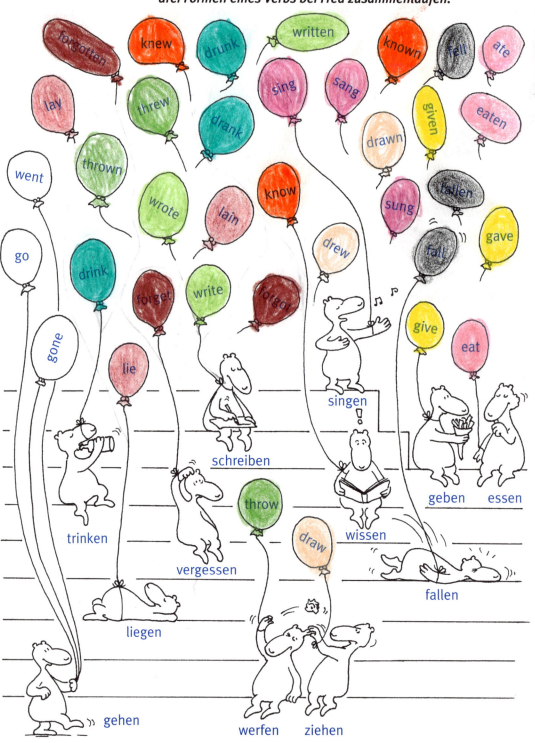

Zeitformen des Verbs

 In der folgenden Tabelle kommen sowohl regelmäßige als auch unregelmäßige Verben in verschiedenen Personen vor. Ergänze die fehlenden Formen:

past perfect	simple past	present perfect	simple present	future
he had played	he played	he has played	he plays	he will play
she had gone	she went	she has gone	she goes	she will go
I had opened	i opened	i have opened	i open	i will open
we had came	we came	we have came	we come	we will come
i had tried	I tried	i have tried	i try	i will try
he had written	he wrote	he has writen	he writes	he will write
she had seen	she saw	she has seen	she sees	she will see
they had spent	they spent	they have spent	they spend	they will spend
she had read	she read	she has read	she read	she will read
it had rained	it rained	it has rained	it rains	it will rain

11

Zeitformen des Verbs

  Hier noch eine Übung für Schnellsprecher. Damit kannst du die Bildung von past perfect *und* simple past *im schnellen Wechsel trainieren.*

Für den Anfang ist es vielleicht hilfreich, wenn du die Sätze anhand der gegebenen Stichwörter aufschreibst. Im zweiten Durchgang kannst du versuchen, die Kettensätze mündlich – und möglichst schnell – zu formulieren.

Here are the clues:

wake up at six – get up – wash – put on my clothes – go downstairs into the kitchen – have breakfast – go into the garden – play football – read a book – write a letter – buy a pound of apples – feed the horses – draw a picture – sing a song – repair the car – watch TV – go to bed

Na, das klappt ja schon ganz prima! Und weil du die Bildung der verschiedenen Zeiten so gut beherrschst, können wir uns jetzt den verneinten Formen und den Fragen zuwenden.

Bei verneinten Sätzen ist in bestimmten Zeiten eine Umschreibung mit *do* nötig.

Vergangenheit		Gegenwart		Zukunft
past perfect	*simple past*	*present perfect*	*simple present*	*future*
she hadn't eaten	she didn't eat	she hasn't eaten	she doesn't eat	she won't eat
we hadn't eaten	we didn't eat	we haven't eaten	we don't eat	we won't eat

Umschreibung mit

didn't **don't/doesn't**

Vervollständige nun die folgende Tabelle:

past perfect	simple past	present perfect	simple present	future
			we don't know	
it hadn't helped				
		she hasn't given		
				you won't win
	I didn't move			
he hadn't forgotten				
				they won't buy
		we haven't seen		
	she didn't spend			
			I don't sleep	

Im Folgenden beschäftigen wir uns mit den Fragesätzen. Hier muss man auf die veränderte Satzstellung achten:

Fragen:

Vergangenheit		Gegenwart		Zukunft
past perfect	simple past	present perfect	simple present	future
had you eaten?	did you eat?	have you eaten?	do you eat?	will you eat?
had she eaten?	did she eat?	has she eaten?	does she eat?	will she eat?

Umschreibung mit *did* ... *do/does*

Zeitformen des Verbs

  Auch Fragen in den verschiedenen Zeiten kannst du wieder mit einer Tabelle üben:

past perfect	simple past	present perfect	simple present	future
			does he like?	
	did you catch?			
had he forgotten?				
				will they go?
		have we hit?		
had they seen?				
				will you tell?
		have I opened?		
			does he take?	
	did she lose?			

Die Verbformen in bejahten und verneinten Sätzen sowie Fragen – wie du sie gerade geübt hast – stellen natürlich nur ein Skelett dar. Jetzt wollen wir versuchen, aus diesen Skeletten richtige Lebewesen entstehen zu lassen, indem wir **ganze Sätze** oder größere Satzzusammenhänge bilden. Dann sehen unsere Verbformen nicht mehr so dürr und klapprig aus!

Zeitformen des Verbs

Du kannst diese Übung schriftlich oder mündlich machen. Suche dir zehn verschiedene Verbformen aus den drei Tabellen aus und mache daraus ganze Sätze oder erzähle eine kleine Geschichte!

Beispiele:

they spent: Our neighbours spent their holidays in the United States. They sent us a postcard on which you can see the Empire State Building.

we haven't seen: We haven't seen our grandparents for more than a year now. They live in Australia.

does he take? Does your son often take things apart? – Yes, he wants to explore everything. But he's not very keen on putting things together again. That's why we can't use our TV set, the toaster, and the hoover[1] at the moment!

[1] Staubsauger

Test

1. Fill in the correct simple past or past perfect forms:
(Je 2 Punkte für jede richtige Form)

A bad day for Mike

Yesterday _____ (not be) Mike's lucky day.

He _____ (forget) to set his alarm clock the night

before, so he _____ (sleep) too long. As he

_____ (not have) time for breakfast he just

_____ (make) himself a sandwich that he

_____ (want) to eat on his way to school.

But then his dog _____ (eat) the sandwich because

Mike _____ (put) it on the kitchen table!

At school he _____ (write) a German test – and of

course he _____ (not revise[1]) the new words.

But on top of all that he _____ (find) out that he

_____ (have) toothpaste on his shirt after he

_____ (talk) to Michelle, the pretty girl who seemed

to fancy[2] him.

[1] to revise – wiederholen

[2] to fancy – hier: gernhaben, mögen

2. Rewrite the sentences, but don't change the tenses.
(Je 2 Punkte für jeden richtigen Satz)

Example:

(bejahter Satz)　　　Michael called me yesterday.
(verneinter Satz)　　Michael didn't call me yesterday.

(Frage)　　　　　　　Will we arrive at the airport in time?
(bejahter Satz)　　　..

(verneinter Satz)　　Judy doesn't get up at five o'clock every day.
(bejahter Satz)　　　..

(Frage)　　　　　　　Have the Greens sold their car?
(verneinter Satz)　　..

(bejahter Satz)　　　Brian has pancakes for breakfast every day.
(verneinter Satz)　　..

(verneinter Satz)　　They hadn't met before.
(Frage)　　　　　　　..

(Frage)　　　　　　　Did Janet buy that dress in New York?
(bejahter Satz)　　　..

Zeitformen des Verbs

Testauswertung

My personal scoreboard:

38–30 "right" scores:
With your excellent result you've won the gold medal!

29–19 "right" scores:
That's a pretty good result! You'll get the silver medal for it! If you want to go for gold, revise the irregular verb forms and/or the tenses you have difficulties with!

18–0 "right" scores:
Maybe you haven't done enough warming-up exercises!
Do all the exercises in this chapter and don't forget to revise the irregular verb forms!

Word Power

Wörter lernen mir Bildern
Pictures and words

In Verbindung mit Bildern bleiben neue Vokabeln viel besser im Gedächtnis haften. Probiere es doch gleich einmal aus! Beschrifte die Zeichnung mithilfe der unten abgedruckten Wörter.

Write the words from the grid next to the picture:

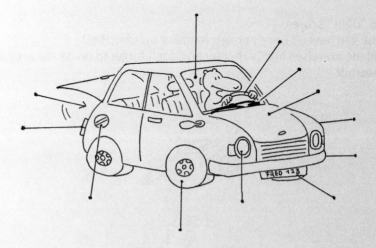

windscreen	bumper	front lights	bonnet
mudguard	boot	petrol tank	tyre
steering wheel	rear lights	number plate	windscreen wipers

After you have written a word next to the picture of the car, say what this part of the car is used for.

Example:

You/We can put your/our luggage or shopping bags into the **boot**.

If you make a photocopy of this page, you can put the picture and the words into an envelope and use them more than once.

Further activities: You can try the same with other pictures.

Here are some suggestions – add more words,
make a photocopy and cut the words out.
Then stick them onto the pictures.

deck-chair	clouds
bathing shorts	sunshade
sunglasses	umbrella
puddle	

You could try to make up little stories. Start like this:

1. A few weeks ago something funny happened. Fred was lying in a deck-chair …
2. Last weekend Fred and some friends of his wanted to go to the cinema. They had just set off when it started to rain …

Englisch reden? – Kein Problem!
Talking in English? – No problem!

1. Jemanden kennenlernen

On the campsite Fred meets a nice Australian girl. Her name is Julie. They ask each other a lot of questions.

B1 *Male die Sprechblasen in verschiedenen Farben an und verwende jeweils die gleiche Farbe für eine Frage und die dazugehörige Antwort. Match the questions and the answers.*

- What's your name?
- Can you play the didgeridoo?[1]
- I'm from Adelaide. That's in the south of Australia.
- Well, I'm quite good at languages, but maths isn't my cup of tea!
- What are your hobbies?
- Alicia Keys is my favourite singer but I also like Australian bands like "Men at Work".
- What kind of music do you like?
- I'm fourteen.
- I like reading, swimming and waterskiing.
- Are you good at school?
- How old are you?
- My name is Fred.
- You mean that traditional Aborigine instrument? No, I'm afraid I can't.
- Where are you from?

What would you answer if somebody asked you all those questions?

Englisch reden

 B2 *Stell dir vor, du lernst im Urlaub ein Mädchen oder einen Jungen kennen, das/der nicht Deutsch spricht. Überlege dir fünf Fragen, die du ihm stellen würdest.*
Lies erst weiter, wenn du diese fünf Fragen formuliert hast!

Vielleicht findest du die eine oder andere deiner Fragen in der folgenden Übung wieder. Ordne die deutschen Formulierungen den englischen Fragen zu:

Wenn du wissen möchtest, ob das Mädchen oder der Junge ...	Wie müsstest du dann fragen?
1. eine(n) Brieffreund(in) hat,	Have you got a pet?
2. gerne Reisen unternimmt,	Would you like to go to the beach?
3. schon mal in Deutschland war,	Have you got school in the afternoon?
4. eine gute Sportlerin/ein guter Sportler ist,	Would you like to keep in touch with me?
5. ein Haustier hat,	Have you ever been to Germany?
6. in einer großen Stadt wohnt,	Are you good at sports?
7. gerne Techno-Musik hört,	Do you like travelling?
8. Geschwister hat,	Have you ever played truant?
9. am Nachmittag Schule hat,	Do you live in a big city?
10. schon mal die Schule geschwänzt hat[1],	Have you got a pen-friend?
11. mit dir zum Strand gehen will,	Do you like listening to Techno music?
12. mit dir in Verbindung bleiben möchte.	Have you got any brothers or sisters?

[1] (to) play truant

Lies die englischen Fragen einige Male laut vor dich hin.
Decke nun die rechte Seite zu und formuliere die entsprechenden Fragen von 1 bis 12.

Englisch reden

Da du dich mit deiner neuen Freundin bzw. deinem neuen Freund prima verstehst, möchtest du sie/ihn auch mal einladen, mit dir etwas zu unternehmen oder sie/ihn um einen Gefallen bitten. Fred zeigt dir, was man in solchen Situationen sagen kann:

Du willst deiner Freundin/deinem Freund vorschlagen, mit dir Tischtennis zu spielen.

Würdest du gerne …?

Wie wär's mit …/ wenn wir …?

Lass uns …!
Spielen wir doch …!

Du bittest sie/ihn, dir etwas zu schicken.

Könnest du bitte …?

Es wäre sehr nett, wenn du …!

Könntest du vielleicht …?

Du möchtest deine Freundin/deinen Freund einladen, dich in den nächsten Ferien zu besuchen.

Warum besuchst du mich nicht …?

Würdest du gerne …?

Ich würde mich sehr freuen, wenn …!

Englisch reden

Für deutsche Muttersprachler wirken derartige Äußerungen im Englischen manchmal übertrieben höflich. Umgekehrt empfinden englische *native speakers* deutsche Sprecher gelegentlich als sehr direkt, barsch oder sogar unhöflich. Sprachliche Umgangsformen sind einfach von Land zu Land verschieden. Deshalb unser Tipp: Drücke dich im Englischen lieber etwas höflicher aus – das verringert die Zahl der Fettnäpfchen, in die man treten kann, ganz beträchtlich!

Beispiel:

Give me the butter! — Ziemlich unhöflich.

Can I have the butter?! — Nicht sehr höflich.

Can I have the butter, please? — Schon besser! Bei Freunden und Familienmitgliedern akzeptabel.

Could / May } *I have the butter, please?* — Höflich.

Could / Would } *you please pass me the butter?!* — Noch höflicher.

Tipp

Englisch reden

 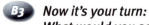 Now it's your turn:
What would you say in the following situations?

1. Du möchtest Freunde zu deiner Geburtstagsfeier einladen.

....

....

¹ etw. ausleihen –
to borrow
jemanden etw. leihen –
to lend

2. Du bittest einen Jungen, dir seine Luftmatratze zu leihen¹.

....

....

3. Du schlägst deinen Eltern vor, nächstes Jahr in Irland Urlaub zu machen.

....

....

4. Du bittest deinen Tischnachbarn, dir das Salz herüberzureichen.

....

....

5. Du schlägst deiner Freundin/deinem Freund vor, abends in die Hotelsdisco zu gehen.

....

....

6. Deine Eltern möchten deine Freundin/deinen Freund und ihre/seine Eltern zum Abendessen einladen.

....

....

Englisch reden

Wenn man jemandem direkt gegenübersteht, ist die Verständigung leichter als am Telefon. Dabei ist Telefonieren in der Fremdsprache gar nicht so schwer, wenn man einige typische Ausdrücke beherrscht!

B4 Fred möchte seinen deutschen Freund Jörg zum Grillen einladen. Die einzelnen Teile des Telefongesprächs sind etwas durcheinander geraten. Kannst du sie in die richtige Reihenfolge (1–12) bringen?

[1] Ich drücke dir die Daumen!

Englisch reden

In dem Gespräch kommen einige typische Ausdrücke vor, die man häufig am Telefon verwendet. Schreibe sie neben die jeweiligen deutschen Übersetzungen:

Hier ist .../Hier spricht ... a) ....
                               b) ....

Kann ich ... sprechen? ....

Bleib dran! ....

Könntest du bitte etwas langsamer sprechen? ....

Wie geht's dir? ....

Mir geht's gut. a) ....
                 b) ....

Hast du am Samstag Zeit? ....

Danke, dass du angerufen hast. ....

Bis Samstag! ....

Auch hier ist wichtig: Lies die Ausdrücke mehrmals laut! Später kannst du als Wiederholung die englischen Ausdrücke zudecken und überprüfen, ob du sie noch alle weißt.

2. Fragen stellen: Welche Fragetypen gibt es?

Im ersten Abschnitt dieses Kapitels hast du geübt, in verschiedenen Gesprächssituationen zurechtzukommen. Es kamen eine ganze Reihe von Fragen vor, die wir jetzt noch einmal genauer unter die Lupe nehmen wollen. Welche Arten von Fragen werden häufig verwendet? Wie werden sie gebildet?

 On Friday evening Fred saw a strange creature in the park. Fred was rather curious. So, instead of running away, he asked the alien some questions:

Complete the dialogue:

_Do_ you understand me?	Yes, I _do_.
_____ I ask you some questions?	Yes, you _____.
_____ you from Mars?	No, I _____.
_____ you come by spacecraft?	No, I _____.
_____ your parents know where you are?	Yes, they _____.
_____ you got any friends here?	Yes, I _____.
_____ you like something to eat?	No, thank you.
_____ you please tell me something about your planet?	Yes, of course.
_____ you go back to your planet soon?	No, I _____.

In fact, I'm going to a fancy-dress party at my friend's house!

Na, man kann sich ja mal irren!

Englisch reden

Freds Fragen fangen zwar alle unterschiedlich an, aber es handelt sich doch immer um den gleichen Fragetyp. Fred hat ausschließlich **Entscheidungsfragen** *(yes/no questions)* gestellt; die Antworten lauten immer „Ja" oder „Nein". Im Englischen steht *Yes* oder *No* fast nie allein, sondern meist als Teil einer sogenannten „Kurzantwort": Das Hilfsverb aus der Frage wird hier wieder aufgegriffen und bejaht oder verneint. Manchmal stehen auch andere Formulierungen wie *Yes, of course* oder *No, thank you*.

Sehen wir uns nun etwas genauer an, wie Entscheidungsfragen gebildet werden.

Can   I   ask you some questions?
Did   you   come by spacecraft?
Have   you   got any friends here?

Wenn nicht schon ein Hilfsverb im Satz vorhanden ist, muss bei Entscheidungsfragen mit *do/does* in der Gegenwart bzw. *did* in der Vergangenheit umschrieben werden.

Zur Erinnerung:
Aussagesatz: **Frage:**

I like pizza.   *Do you like pizza?*
Peter likes pancakes.   *Does Peter like pancakes?*

In der **3. Person Singular** steht **in der Gegenwart** ein **-s**!

They came by train.   *Did they come by train?*
Bob came by train.   *Did Bob come by train?*

Das **Verb** steht bei Fragen mit *do/does/did* immer in der Grundform.

Exercise

 Formuliere Entscheidungsfragen mit Do …? / Does …? *oder* Did …?

1. Jack/live/in London — Does Jack live in London?
2. I/lock/the door/last night
3. your brother/speak/Italian
4. you/go out/last Saturday
5. the Millers/spend their holidays/in Florida/last year
6. you/always/get up/so early
7. your parents/like/dogs
8. Jenny/do well/in her last English test

Englisch reden

Game

Für das folgende Ratespiel benötigst du eine(n) oder mehrere Mitspieler(innen).

One of the players chooses

a person,   **an animal,**   **a thing,**   **or a place.**

The other player(s) have to ask questions in order to find out what it is.

Here is an example: Mike starts: O. K., I've got it – it's a thing.

Judy:	Have you got it in your house?	Yes, we have.
Fred:	Is it bigger than a football?	No, it isn't.
Judy:	Do you need it for school?	No, I don't.
Fred:	Is it a toy?	No, it isn't.
Judy:	Is it part of the furniture?	No, it isn't.
Fred:	Can you eat it?	No, you can't!
Judy:	Has everybody got such a thing in the house?	Yes, almost everybody.
Fred:	Do you need it for cooking or eating?	No, you don't.
Judy:	Do you have it in the bathroom?	Yes, I do.
	Is it a toothbrush?	Bingo! Yes, it is.
		Now it's your turn!

29

Englisch reden

Bisher hatten wir es immer mit Entscheidungsfragen zu tun. Es gibt aber noch eine weitere wichtige Gruppe von Fragen, die darauf abzielen, dass der Fragende bestimmte Informationen erhält – **Fragesätze mit Fragepronomen**, zum Beispiel:

> **Fragepronomen:** *how long – how many – who (wer) – who (wen) – what – when – where – what colour – what kind of – why – how often – how much*

  Fill in the right pronoun:
Der berühmte Detektiv Frederic Holmes führt gerade wichtige Ermittlungen durch.

_____ is that man? – Charles Breakneck!

_____ did you last see him? – Last Friday.

_____ was that? – In the Penguin Bar.

_____ was he wearing? – A coat, I think.

_____ coat? – A leather coat.

_____ ? – Black.

_____ did he stay there? – The whole evening, until one o'clock, I think.

_____ money did he spend there? – I don't know, but I'm sure it was more than £ 100.

_____ people were there that night? – Oh, it was quite crowded, more than 50, I think.

_____ do you normally go there? – Twice a week.

_____ do you go there? – I like the atmosphere. And I like to meet people.

_____ do you meet there? – Friends.

Englisch reden

> Auch **für Fragesätze mit Fragepronomen** gilt:
> Sätze, in denen kein Hilfsverb vorkommt, werden in der Regel mit *do/does/did* umschrieben.

Achtung bei *Who/What ...?*

Who did you meet last Friday? Fragt man mit *Who ...?* oder *What ...?*
(Wen hast du ... getroffen?) nach dem **Objekt,** wird wie gewohnt
What did you see? mit *do/does/did* umschrieben.
(Was hast du gesehen?)

Who knows that man? Fragt man mit *Who ...?* oder *What ...?*
(Wer kennt ...?) nach dem **Subjekt,** wird **nicht** mit
What stands in the middle of ...? *do/does/did* umschrieben.
(Was steht ...?)

B8 *Frage nach den unterstrichenen Satzteilen.*

Beispiel: <u>Ann</u> met <u>Richard</u> at a party.   a) Who met Richard at a party?
b) Who did Anne meet at a party?

1. <u>A fifteen-year-old boy</u> saw <u>the two robbers</u> at Victoria Station.
   a) ......
   b) ......

2. <u>The apple</u> hit <u>my teacher</u> on the head.
   a) ......
   b) ......

3. <u>All the pupils</u> like <u>Mrs Brown</u>.
   a) ......
   b) ......

4. <u>Helen</u> often sees <u>flying saucers</u> in her garden.
   a) ......
   b) ......

5. <u>Judith</u> loves <u>Matthew</u>.
   a) ......
   b) ......

Englisch reden

  In den folgenden Übungen sind alle Fragetypen vertreten, die du bisher geübt hast.
Hast du Lust, dich mal als Krimiautor zu versuchen? Frederic Holmes arbeitet an einem neuen Fall. Formuliere seine Fragen und erfinde Antworten dazu. Schreibe den Dialog auf ein gesondertes Blatt.

Holmes will von einem wichtigen Zeugen wissen,

wo er wohnt,
wo er gestern Abend war,
wer ihn dort gesehen hat,
wie lange er dort geblieben ist,
wo sein Autoschlüssel ist,
ob er die Frau auf dem Foto kennt,
wo sie wohnt,
wann er sie zum letzten Mal gesehen hat.

3. Seine Meinung äußern

In einer „normalen" Unterhaltung stellt man nicht nur Fragen bzw. gibt Antworten; man tauscht auch Erfahrungen und Gedanken aus. So wie die beiden Teenager, die sich gerade über das Fernsehen unterhalten:

 Es gehören je eine Äußerung und eine Erwiderung zusammen. Verbinde sie mit einer Linie oder male die zusammengehörenden Sprechblasen mit der gleichen Farbe aus.
Connect the statement and the reply that go to together.

[1] sitcom: situation comedy – lustige Familienserie
[2] ugs. Glotze

Englisch reden

Hier findest du einige Ausdrücke, mit deren Hilfe du deine Meinung bzw. Zustimmung oder Widerspruch äußern kannst:

So äußerst du deine Meinung:

If you ask me ...	Wenn du mich fragst ...
I think ...	Ich denke/meine ...
What I think is that ...	Ich meine, dass ...
In my opinion ...	Meiner Meinung nach ...
I'm sure (that) ...	Ich bin mir sicher, (dass) ...
As far as I know ...	Soviel ich weiß ...
I'm (absolutely) convinced that ...	Ich bin (absolut) überzeugt, dass ...

So stimmst du deinem Gesprächspartner zu:

That's right/true.	Das stimmt. Das ist richtig/wahr.
I think so, too.	Das denke ich auch.
That's just what I think.	Genau das denke ich auch.
Yes, of course.	Ja, natürlich.
So do I.	Ich auch.
Neither do I.	Ich auch nicht.
Exactly.	Stimmt genau.
I agree with you.	Ich bin deiner Meinung.
That's a good point/idea.	Das ist ein gutes Argument/ein guter Gedanke.

So widersprichst du deinem Gesprächspartner:

O. K., but don't you think ...?	Gut, aber meinst du nicht ...?
Yes, but on the other hand ...	Ja, aber andererseits ...
I'm sorry but I don't agree.	Es tut mir leid, aber ich bin nicht deiner Meinung.
I don't think so.	Ich sehe das anders.
That's not true.	Das stimmt nicht.
I just can't agree with you.	Da kann ich dir einfach nicht zustimmen!
On the contrary ...	Im Gegenteil ...
Come on!	Ach geh!
Rubbish!	Quatsch! Blödsinn!

Englisch reden

  Now it's your turn.
Comment on the following statements:

It's good to learn a foreign language.	No family should have more than one car.	Fast food is unhealthy.
German television is excellent.	Homework is necessary.	Riding a motorbike is dangerous.
Girls shouldn't play football.	German pupils should wear school uniforms.	Women should get equal pay for equal work.

 Aus dieser Übung wird ein spannendes Lernspiel, wenn du einen Mitspieler/eine Mitspielerin findest.
Kennst du *Tic-Tac-Toe*? Das ist ein Spiel und geht so:

Ein Mitspieler/eine Mitspielerin malt Kreuze, der/die andere malt Kreise. Es wird ausgelost, wer anfangen darf. Das Gitter ist zunächst leer. Der erste Spieler setzt sein Zeichen in eines der neun Felder; dann ist der andere Spieler dran. Ziel ist es, eine Dreierreihe (senkrecht, waagerecht oder diagonal) vollzubekommen.
Die Spieler dürfen ihr Symbol erst setzen, wenn sie etwas zu der Äußerung gesagt haben, die in dem betreffenden Feld steht!

Beim nächsten Durchgang fängt der andere Mitspieler an. Ihr könnt euch natürlich andere Äußerungen/Behauptungen überlegen – dann lässt sich das Spiel beliebig oft wiederholen. Und nicht vergessen: Erst nach einer vollständigen, richtigen Äußerung darf ein Kreuz bzw. Kreis gesetzt werden!

Englisch reden

B12 *Zum Abschluss ein kleines Streitgespräch. Übersetze, was sich die beiden Kontrahenten zu sagen haben:*

School holidays are too long!

1. Meiner Meinung nach sind drei Monate Schulferien zu lang!

   ....
   ....
   ....

2. Da bin ich anderer Ansicht! Kinder und Jugendliche brauchen diese Zeit, um sich zu erholen.

   ....
   ....
   ....

3. Soviel ich weiß, schlafen (doch) die meisten Schüler im Unterricht. Ich finde, das reicht!

   ....
   ....
   ....

4. Das finde ich aber nicht! Ein Schultag ist wirklich anstrengend, und danach müssen die Schüler (noch) ihre Hausaufgaben machen.

   ....
   ....
   ....

5. Ach was! Es ist keine Schule am Wochenende, und alle paar Wochen sind Ferien. Die Kids wissen doch gar nicht, was sie mit ihrer Freizeit anfangen sollen.

   ....
   ....
   ....

6. Das stimmt nicht. Wir brauchen einfach Zeit für unsere Familie, Freunde und Hobbys. Ich bin mir sicher, dass Sie auch nicht jeden Tag arbeiten wollen!

   ....
   ....
   ....

Bestimmt bist du jetzt mit uns der Meinung: Englisch reden – kein Problem! Den abschließenden Test schaffst du sicher mühelos!

Englisch reden

Test

1. Frage Pete,
(Je 2 Punkte für jede richtige Frage)

1. ob er Amerikaner ist.
2. wann er morgens aufsteht.
3. wo er wohnt.
4. ob er dir sein Fahrrad leihen könnte.
5. was er letzten Samstag getan hat.
6. wer „Frankenstein" geschrieben hat.
7. ob er schon mal auf Malta war.
8. wo sein Bruder arbeitet.

2. Übersetze die folgenden Äußerungen zum Thema: School uniforms
(Je 2 Punkte für jede richtige Äußerung)

1. Soviel ich weiß, sind die meisten Schuluniformen dunkelblau, grau oder dunkelgrün.
2. Meiner Meinung nach sollte jeder selbst entscheiden können, was er/sie anziehen will.
3. Genau das denke ich auch. Wenn du mich fragst: Schuluniformen sehen langweilig aus.
4. Ja, aber andererseits ist die Schule keine Disco! Viele Mädchen und Jungs verbringen Stunden vor dem Kleiderschrank!
5. Da stimme ich dir voll zu! Für viele Kids sind Klamotten extrem wichtig – zu wichtig!

Testauswertung

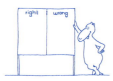

My personal scoreboard:

26–20 "right" scores:
Congratulations! Talking in English is no problem at all for you.

19–13 "right" scores:
Well done! You just need a little more practice. Revise the aspects of conversation you still find difficult.

12–0 "right" scores:
Are you being serious? Have you done **all** the exercises in this chapter? Well, then – off you go! You will see: practice makes perfect!

Word Power

Nachschlagen im Wörterbuch I
How to use the dictionary I

Bestimmt hast du diese Erfahrung auch schon gemacht: Du willst etwas auf Englisch sagen oder schreiben, aber du weißt ein bestimmtes Wort nicht.

Auch wenn du kein Wörterbuch zur Hand hast, solltest du nicht verzweifeln. Du kannst versuchen, das Wort zu umschreiben, das dir fehlt. Mehr dazu auf den Word power-Seiten *Nie wieder sprachlos*.

Manchmal hast du aber mehr Zeit, z. B. wenn du deine Hausaufgaben machst oder einen Brief schreibst, und kannst im Wörterbuch nachschlagen. Oder du willst einfach wissen, wie das Wort nun eigentlich auf Englisch heißt, das du in der Unterhaltung so dringend gebraucht hättest.

Jetzt wollen wir Antje, die das Wort für **Gänge beim Fahrrad** sucht, tatkräftig unterstützen. In einem Wörterbuch kommen immer wieder bestimmte Abkürzungen, Symbole und Zeichen vor, und es ist sehr wichtig, ihre Bedeutung zu kennen. Hier der Wörterbucheintrag zu **Gang**:

Gang 1. (≈ *Gangart*) walk; **seine Gangart** the way he walks **2.** (≈ *Weg*) way **3.** (≈ *Flur*) corridor **4.** *im Flugzeug usw.*: aisle [⚠ aɪl] **5.** (≈ *Bogengang*) arcade [ɑːˈkeɪd] **6.** *beim Essen*: course [kɔːs]; **Essen mit drei Gängen** three-course meal **7.** *beim Auto*: gear [gɪə]; **zweiter** *usw.* **Gang** second *usw.* gear; **in den zweiten Gang schalten** change (*bes. AE* shift) into second (gear) **8.** *anatomisch*: duct, canal [kəˈnæl] **9.** (≈ *Verlauf*) course; **der Gang der Dinge** the course of events **10. etwas in Gang setzen** (*oder* **bringen**) *wörtlich und übertragen* get* something going, start something **11. in Gang kommen** get* going, get* started **12. es ist etwas im Gange übertragen** there's something going on **13. die Feier war in vollem Gange, als ...** the party was in full swing when ... [1]

- Stichwort
- Warndreieck, z. B. bei komplizierter Aussprache
- verschiedene Bedeutungen
- Sternchen beim unregelmäßigen Verb
- kursiv: Verständnishilfen
- entspricht
- Amerikanisches Englisch (BE = Britisches Englisch)
- Aussprache
- halbfett kursiv: Wendungen

[1] aus: Langenscheidts Power Dictionary Englisch, Berlin, München 2004

Das Wort **Gang** hat viele verschiedene Bedeutungen, aus denen wir einige wichtige herausgreifen wollen. Trage die passende englische Übersetzung ein:

1. Gangart ....
2. Weg ....
3. Flur ....
4. im Flugzeug ....
5. beim Essen ....
6. beim Auto und Fahrrad ....
7. Verlauf ....

Now look up the following words and write down the English translations:

Bitte gib mir die Karte.	Postkarte	....
Please, give me the ...	Landkarte	....
	Fahrkarte	....
	Speisekarte	....
Das ist der letzte Zug.	Eisenbahn	....
This is the last ...	Schachzug	....
Ich kann das Rezept nicht finden.	Kochrezept	....
I can't find the ...	Rezept vom Arzt	....
Er sitzt schon seit Stunden auf dieser Bank.	Geldinstitut	....
He has been sitting on this ... for hours.	Sitzbank	....
Ist dieses Bild von Picasso?	allgemein	....
Is that a ... by Picasso?	Gemälde	....
	Foto	....
	Zeichnung	....

Die Verwendung von past tense und present perfect
The use of the past tense and the present perfect

Angler catches whale

Mr J. Gallagher, a 43-year-old taxi driver from Stonehaven, was fishing off the pier last Saturday. When he wanted to reel in[1] a fish, he got the shock of his life: he had caught a dead whale which had been drifting[2] in the sea!
"It took me about 45 minutes to pull the whale ashore[3]", Mr Gallagher told our reporter. "I got help from some passers-by[4]. You know, I've been going fishing for more than fifteen years now, but this is the biggest 'fish' I've ever caught!"
As we were told by a marine expert, the whale is 20 feet[5] long. So far nobody knows what caused the death of the whale.

[1] (die Angelschnur) einholen
[2] treiben
[3] an Land
[4] Passanten, Vorübergehende
[5] ca. 6,10 Meter

Auch in diesem Kapitel stehen verschiedene Zeiten – nämlich das *past tense* und *present perfect* – im Mittelpunkt. Falls du dir nicht mehr ganz sicher bist, wie diese Zeiten gebildet werden, empfehlen wir dir, zunächst Kapitel A dieses Buches durchzuarbeiten.
Solltest du das bereits getan haben, kannst du gleich mit der ersten Übung loslegen:

Past tense und present perfect

  In dem Zeitungsbericht über den kuriosen Walfang kommen die folgenden Zeiten mindestens einmal vor. Trage in jede Spalte ein Beispiel aus dem Text ein:

past perfect (simple): ....

past perfect (progressive): ....

past (simple): ....

past (progressive): ....

present perfect (simple): ....

present perfect (progressive): ....

1. *Simple past* und *present perfect*

Nehmen wir noch einmal unseren Zeitstrahl zu Hilfe, um das *simple past* und das *present perfect* voneinander abzugrenzen:

Vergangenheit	Gegenwart
When Mr Linnane wanted to reel in a fish, he got the shock of his life!	This is the biggest "fish" I've ever caught!

> Wenn ein Vorgang oder eine Handlung eindeutig in der Vergangenheit passierte, steht das *past tense*.
> Das *present perfect* bildet eine Brücke zwischen Vergangenheit und Gegenwart.

Diese Regeln gelten auch für die jeweilige *progressive form*:

Vergangenheit	Gegenwart
Mr Linnane was fishing off the promenade last Thursday.	I've been going fishing for 15 years now.

Past tense und present perfect

Es gibt einige **Signalwörter**, die es dir noch leichter machen, dich für die richtige Zeitform zu entscheiden:

simple past		*present perfect*	
last week	letzte Woche	up to now	
yesterday	gestern	until now	bisher,
two years ago	vor zwei Jahren	till now	bis jetzt
when I was ...	als ich ... war	yet (in ver-	
when (in Fragen)	wann	neinten Sätzen)	noch nicht
in 1996	(im Jahr) 1996	yet (in Fragen)	schon
		for	seit (Zeitraum)
		since	seit (Zeitpunkt)

> **Aufgepasst!**
> Im Deutschen steht in der Umgangssprache bei Erzählungen oft das Perfekt, im Englischen dagegen das simple past.

Gestern **habe** ich mit meinem Freund Pete Tennis **gespielt**.

Die Handlung – das Tennismatch – gehört eindeutig der **Vergangenheit** an, deshalb muss im Englischen *simple past* stehen:

*Yesterday I **played** tennis with my friend Pete.*

Past tense und present perfect

Exercise C2

Zwei Mädchen unterhalten sich über die Ferien, die eine von den beiden in Spanien verbracht hat.
Ergänze die englischen Verbformen und vergiss dabei nicht, dass du bei Berichten über Vergangenes immer das past tense verwenden musst:

Wo seid ihr denn in den Ferien gewesen?

Wir waren in Spanien.

War's schön?

Ja. Wir hatten ein schönes Ferienhaus in der Nähe des Strandes. Vormittags haben wir oft etwas besichtigt und nachmittags sind wir dann an den Strand gegangen und haben Volleyball gespielt oder im Meer gebadet.

Hast du auch nette Leute getroffen?

Ja, da war eine Familie aus Hamburg mit zwei Mädchen. Die eine war 14, die andere 12. Wir haben viel zusammen gemacht.

Wie war das Essen?

Wir haben meistens selbst gekocht. Alle paar Tage sind wir in ein Restaurant gegangen und haben etwas typisch Spanisches gegessen. Nur einmal hatte ich etwas, das mir nicht geschmeckt hat. Sonst war es immer sehr lecker.

Ach, übrigens – vielen Dank für deine Karte! Ich hab sie gestern bekommen.

Erst gestern? Ich hab sie vor mehr als zwei Wochen geschrieben!

– Where *(spend)* .... your holidays?
– We *(be)* .... in Spain.
– *(be)* .... it nice?
– Yes, it was./We *(have)* .... a nice holiday home near the beach. In the morning we often *(visit)* .... some sights and in the afternoon we *(go)* .... to the beach and *(play)* .... volleyball or *(swim)* .... in the sea.
– *(meet)* .... any nice people?
– Yes, there *(be)* .... a family from Hamburg with two girls. One *(be)* .... 14, the other one *(be)* .... 12. We *(do)* .... a lot of things together.
– What *(be)* .... the food like?
– Most of the time we *(cook)* .... our own meals. Every few days we *(go)* .... to a restaurant and *(eat)* .... some typical Spanish food. Only once I *(have)* .... something I *(not like)* .... Apart from that it *(be)* .... always very tasty.
– By the way – many thanks for your postcard! I *(get)* .... it yesterday.
– Only yesterday? I *(write)* .... it more than two weeks ago!

Past tense und present perfect

Nachdem du den Lückentext ausgefüllt hast, lies nun den ganzen (englischen) Text noch einmal durch, decke ihn dann ab und versuche den gesamten Dialog ins Englische zu übersetzen. Und nicht vergessen: immer *past tense*!

Jetzt wollen wir noch einen Blick auf die Verwendung des *present perfect* werfen:

> **Regel**
>
> Hier wird eine **allgemeine Frage** gestellt bzw. eine **allgemeine Aussage** gemacht – und zwar **ohne genaue Zeitangabe**.
> Wenn das **Ergebnis** im Vordergrund steht, verwendet man das *present perfect*.

Past tense und present perfect

Exercise Dazu gleich eine Übung:

At a travel agency

Now go on. The following expressions will help you:

spend some weeks in New York – climb Mount Everest – sail across the Atlantic Ocean – watch kiwis in New Zealand – fly to Japan – cross the Sahara desert on the back of a camel – ~~be on safari in Africa~~

Past tense und present perfect

Past tense und present perfect

Fassen wir die letzten beiden Übungen noch einmal zusammen:

| allgemeine Aussage (Zeitpunkt nicht genannt) *often, never, ... ever ...?* etc. | ⇒ | *present perfect* |

| zeitlich genau festgelegte Handlung in der Vergangenheit (Zeitpunkt genannt) *... ago, yesterday, last ...* etc. | ⇒ | *simple past* |

Have you ever been to England, Scotland, Wales or Ireland? And have you ever had a real "English breakfast" there?

Well, this is what a real English breakfast looks like:

English breakfast

<u>Grapefruit or juice</u> (orange, grapefruit, tomato)
* * *
<u>Cereals</u>: porridge, cornflakes, all bran, rice crispies
* * *
<u>Cooked dishes</u>: bacon or sausages or kippers[1],
two eggs (fried [2], boiled [3] or poached[4]),
fried bread or toast, baked beans or fried tomato
* * *
<u>Toast, breakfast rolls or croissants</u> with butter, marmalade, jam
<u>Tea, coffee, milk</u>

[1] geräucherter Hering
[2] gebraten = Spiegelei
[3] gekocht
[4] pochiert = „verlorenes" Ei

By the way – English, Scottish, Welsh or Irish people don't have such a big breakfast every day! But for tourists it's a "must"!

Past tense und present perfect

 Tobias is in England for the first time. After two days in London he and his classmates spend a fortnight¹ with English families. It's his first morning with the Stones in Wigan.

¹ 14 Tage

Mrs Stone: Have you ever had grapefruit juice before?
(have)

Tobias: *have/often* Yes, I have often had it.

buy/last week My mother bought a bottle last week.

Mrs Stone: Have _____ ?
(eat)

Tobias: *eat/last week* Yes, I _____ it on the boat _____ .

bacon and eggs

Mrs Stone: _____ ?
(drink)

Tobias: *drink/yet* No, I _____

yesterday/have _____ in London I _____ coffee.

English tea

Mrs Stone: _____ ?
(taste)

Tobias: *have/often* I _____ them at home.

grilled sausages

try/never But I _____ them for breakfast. And I think they are different in Germany.

Mrs Stone: _____ ?
(eat)

Tobias: *eat/never* Sugar puffs? No!

I _____ them before. But I would like to try them.

47

Past tense und present perfect

2. *Simple past* und *past progressive*

I was having a shower when the doorbell rang.

 Das *past progressive* hat einen länger andauernden Vorgang in der Vergangenheit zum Inhalt. Häufig beschreibt es eine Art **Hintergrundhandlung**, die gerade im Verlauf, d. h. noch nicht zu Ende war, als etwas Neues *(simple past!)* passierte.

Auf unserem Zeitstrahl würde das so aussehen:

when the doorbell rang
↓

I was having a shower

  Fred wasn't the only one who was having a shower. Fill in the correct past progressive forms:

1. Cathy to her sister Sabrina: I *was having* a shower when someone switched off the light!
   Sabrina: Oops – I'm sorry. I didn't know you .... a shower. I thought it was Dad!
2. Frank .... a shower when someone opened the door, ran towards him and jumped at him. – It was his dog Prince!
3. Tom: While we .... a shower after the match, our coach was still outside on the field. He couldn't believe that we had actually won.
4. While the girls .... a shower, some boys tried to peep through the keyhole. But the sports teacher caught them and they got into real trouble!

Past tense und present perfect

C6 *What were they doing when it started to rain?*

1. Tom and Judy ....
2. The Johnsons ....
3. Fred ....

4. Mr Greenfield ....
5. Linda, Joan and Kevin ....
6. Our neighbour's cat ....

C7 *In der folgenden Übung musst du entscheiden, wann du es mit einer Hintergrundhandlung und wann mit einer neu einsetzenden Handlung zu tun hast.*

Simple past or *past progressive*? Fill in the correct verb form:

1. The pupils .... (throw) scraps¹ of paper at each   ¹ Fetzen
   other when the teacher .... (come) in.
2. While the Barristers .... (have) dinner, there
   .... (be) a knock at the door.
3. Sally .... (eat) a banana when a monkey suddenly
   .... (jump) on her shoulder.
4. The lights .... (go) out while we
   .... (play) cards.
5. While Sherlock Holmes, the famous detective, ...
   (look) at some pictures, he .... (have) an idea.
6. Fred .... (read) a ghost story when he suddenly
   .... (hear) footsteps.

Past tense und present perfect

3. Der Gebrauch des *present perfect* mit *since* und *for*

Poor Fred is seriously ill! He has got ...

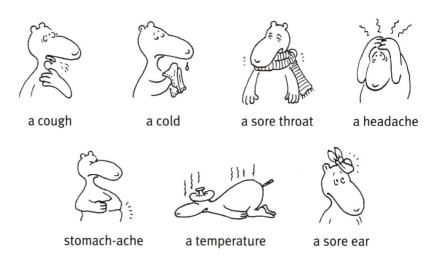

He has to see the doctor:

! Das englische *present perfect* schlägt eine Brücke zwischen Vergangenheit und Gegenwart: Freds Halsschmerzen fingen vor zwei Tagen an, und er hat sie jetzt immer noch.
Im Deutschen verwendet man in diesem Fall das Präsens (die Gegenwart) – wie du siehst.

Past tense und present perfect

Vielleicht ist dir noch etwas aufgefallen:

... *for* two days.   ... seit zwei Tagen
... *since* yesterday   ... seit gestern

Für das deutsche „seit" gibt es im Englischen zwei Übersetzungsmöglichkeiten:

for und *since*

Aber wann verwendet man nun das eine, wann das andere?

Das folgende Schaubild wird dir Klarheit verschaffen:

Fred has had a toothache ...

***since** Friday.*

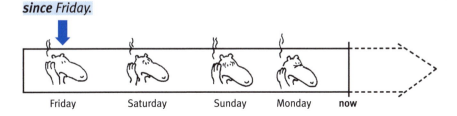

Beginn der Handlung: Zeitpunkt

***for** four days.*

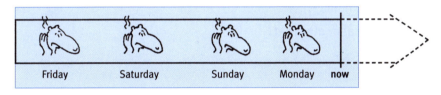

Dauer der Handlung: Zeitspanne

Past tense und present perfect

Wird der **Anfang** der Handlung genannt, steht im Englischen *since*:
since yesterday, since 3 o'clock, since 2005, since last Christmas.

Wird die **Dauer** der Handlung genannt, steht im Englischen *for*:
for two days, for a month, for three hours, for a while, for ages.

  Nun antworte für Fred:

How long have you had ...

... your headache? .... three days.
... your stomach-ache? .... two hours.
... a sore ear? .... last Tuesday.
... a sore throat? .... yesterday.
... your cold? .... two weeks.

 C9 *Some personal questions: Answer with* **since** *or* **for.**

How long have you had ...

... this book?
... your bicycle?
... your watch?
... your school bag?
... your cassette recorder?

And how long have you and your family had ...

... your car?
... your flat or house?
... your dog, cat or other pet?
... your _____ ?
... your _____ ?

Past tense und present perfect

Auch das *present perfect progressive* steht häufig in Verbindung mit *since* oder *for*:

C10 *Kannst du Fred wieder helfen, die fehlenden Formen des* present perfect progressive *zu ergänzen?*

I have been waiting for him …

you	....	for him …
he/she	....	for him …
we	....	for him …
you	....	for him …
they	....	for him …

Das *present perfect progressive* wird verwendet, wenn es sich um einen länger andauernden Vorgang handelt, der **in der Vergangenheit begonnen hat** und **in der Gegenwart noch andauert**.

Past tense und present perfect

Exercise C11 How long have they been doing it?

1. work in the garden/this morning
   Mr Brown has been working in the garden since this morning.

2. wash her car/five o'clock
   Carol

3. watch TV/half an hour
   Ann

4. read the newspaper/breakfast
   Tom's grandpa

5. write a letter/she came home from school
   Susan

6. prepare the dinner/two hours
   Mr Standish

7. suffer from stomach-ache/he ate that lovely cake
   Fred

8. play chess/three hours
   Tom and Peter

Past tense und present perfect

Nachdem du die Verwendung von *past tense* und *present perfect* intensiv geübt hast, zum Abschluss unser Test:

Test

Übersetze ins Englische.
(Je 3 Punkte für jeden richtigen Satz. Punkteabzug bei Wortfehlern und falschen Verbformen)

Some tourists in London

1. Wir warten hier (schon) seit zwei Stunden!

2. Ich war noch nie im Tower von London – und jetzt ist er geschlossen!

3. Hast du diesen Hut gestern auf dem Portobello Market gekauft?

Past tense und present perfect

Testauswertung

My personal scoreboard:

18–14 "right" scores:
Excellent! Fred wouldn't have done better!

13–9 "right" scores:
Well done, indeed! If there is a tense you still have problems with – revise that part of the chapter. Then you won't have any difficulties in the future!

8–0 "right" scores:
Maybe you haven't read this chapter carefully enough. Do all the exercises – then you will be more successful!

Word Power

Hören und Sprechen
Listening and speaking

Eine gute englische Aussprache ist – wie so vieles – Trainingssache. Für ein Erfolg versprechendes Aussprachetraining brauchst du:
- eine besprochene Übungs-CD bzw. Kassette (gibt es zu den meisten Lehrwerken und zu vielen Lektüren),
- ein ruhiges Plätzchen und
- die Bereitschaft, gut zuzuhören.

(Auch im Internet kannst du Ausspracheübungen herunterladen.)

1. Nachsprechübung
Höre dir einen Dialog oder Hörtext immer erst ganz an. Beim zweiten Durchgang stoppst du nach jedem Satz oder Sinnabschnitt und versuchst, das Gehörte möglichst genau nachzusprechen. Nimm das von dir Gesprochene mit dem Mikro auf und vergleich es mit dem Original.

2. Rollenspiel
In vielen Dialogen kommen typische Redewendungen vor, die man in einer bestimmten Situation verwendet (z. B. beim Einkaufen). Es ist äußerst sinnvoll, sich solche Ausdrücke besonders gut einzuprägen. Dafür konzentrierst du dich auf eine Person in dem betreffenden Dialog. Sprich nur nach, was diese Person sagt, und wiederhole diese Nachsprechübung noch ein- bis zweimal. Dann übernimmst du die Rolle – das Drehbuch kennst du ja nun schon! Drücke auf Pause, bevor die bewusste Person zu Wort kommt, und sprich – wie ein Schauspieler – deinen Part.

3. Der kleine Unterschied
Achte beim Zuhören und Sprechen auch auf scheinbare Kleinigkeiten. Sie können mitunter ganz schön wichtig sein.

Hörst du den Unterschied? Probiere selbst:

d oder *t*?   be......... (Bett), be......... (Wette, wetten)
.........ie (binden, Krawatte), ...ie (sterben)
ten......... (Zelt), ten......... (neigen)

b oder *p*?   ....ath (Bad), ...ath (Pfad, Weg)
.........ack (packen), ...ack (Rücken, zurück)
.........ig (Schwein), ...ig (groß)

g oder *c*?   ....uard (Wächter), ...ard (Karte)
.........oat (Mantel), ...oat (Ziege)
.........ame (kam), ...ame (Spiel)

4. Rappen kann jeder!
Aus so manchem Dialog bzw. Text oder aus so mancher Übung lässt sich ein fetziger Rap machen. Du schlägst damit gleich mehrere Fliegen mit einer Klappe:
– du trainierst deine Aussprache,
– du prägst dir bestimmte Strukturen ein und
– du kannst mal so richtig zeigen, was du draufhast!
Übrigens: Zu zweit oder zu dritt wird das Ganze noch lustiger.

Halte Augen und Ohren offen – bestimmt findest du dann jede Menge Texte, die sich für einen *Rap* eignen!
Coole Raps zum Englischlernen als CD oder zum Downloaden gibt es auch bei mentor:
– VERB RAPS, Englische Verben
– PREPOSITION RAPS, Englische Präpositionen
– RIGHT OR WRONG? RAPS, Englische Stolpersteine

Can, must, may – und ihre Ersatzformen
Can, must, may – and their substitutes

Ich konnte nicht früher kommen. Ich musste mein Fahrrad reparieren.

I couldn't come earlier. I had to repair my bike.

Im Unterschied zum Deutschen können die modalen Hilfsverben *can*, *must* und *may* (können, müssen, dürfen) nicht alle Zeiten bilden. Deshalb heißen sie auch „unvollständige" Hilfsverben. Aber zum Glück gibt es Ersatzformen, die in allen Zeiten zum Einsatz kommen können! Apropos „können":

1. Das unvollständige Hilfsverb *can*

Tommy is now 18 months old.

He **can**
- say "Mummy" and "Daddy".
- walk without any help.
- switch on the radio.
- drink from a cup.
- build a tower with his bricks.

You can also say: He **is able to** say "Mummy" and "Daddy".

 Read the sentences aloud and use **is able to** instead of **can**.

Exercise

können	*can/be able to*
(fähig sein, etwas zu tun)	
Ich kann schwimmen.	*I can swim. I'm able to swim.*
Er kann schwimmen.	*He can swim. He is able to swim.*

Can, must, may

Exercise

D2 *Last year Tommy was only six months old.*

He **couldn't** say "Mummy" and "Daddy".
He **couldn't** ...

Say what Tommy **couldn't** do when he was only six months old.

Instead of couldn't (could not) you can also say:

He **wasn't (was not) able to** say ...
He **wasn't able to** ...

Now say what Tommy **wasn't able to** do when he was only six months old.

Hier noch einmal das Hilfsverb „können" (fähig/in der Lage sein) im Überblick:

		Ersatzform:
ich kann schwimmen	*I can swim*	*I'm able to swim*
ich kann nicht schwimmen	*I cannot/can't swim*	*I'm not able to swim*
ich konnte schwimmen	*I could swim*	*I was able to swim*
ich konnte nicht schwimmen	*I could not/ couldn't swim*	*I was not able to swim* *I wasn't able to swim*

Can hat zwar eine Vergangenheitsform *(could)*, aber in allen anderen Zeiten musst du auf die Ersatzform *be able to* zurückgreifen. Dazu später mehr.

Neben der Bedeutung „fähig sein, etwas zu tun" hat *can* noch eine weitere:

„Kann ich mit Fred zum Schwimmen gehen?" Hier heißt „können" so viel wie „dürfen". Und in diesem Fall hat *can* dann auch eine andere Ersatzform: *be allowed to*.

Can, must, may

		Ersatzform:
können (fähig/in der Lage sein, etw. zu tun)	can	be able to
können (dürfen)	can	be allowed to

 In der folgenden Übung geht es darum, die beiden Bedeutungen von can auseinanderzuhalten und die richtige Ersatzform zu verwenden.

Beispiel:
Wir konnten von unserem Hotelzimmer aus die Rocky Mountains sehen.

We _could_ / _were able to_ see the Rocky Mountains from our hotel room.

1. Meine Brieffreundin Fiona kann ein bisschen Deutsch sprechen.

   My penfriend Fiona _____ speak a little German.

2. Ich kann nicht mit zum Konzert gehen. Meine Eltern erlauben es nicht.

   I _____ go to the concert with you. ...

3. Das Nilpferd konnte mit vier Bällen jonglieren.

   The hippo _____ juggle with four balls.

4. Simon hat seine Eltern gefragt – er kann mit uns zum Zelten fahren.

   ... – he _____ go camping with us.

5. Auf den Autobahnen konnte man nicht mehr als 70 Meilen pro Stunde fahren.

   On the motorways you _____ drive more than 70 mph[1].   [1] miles per hour

Damit sind wir schon beim nächsten unvollständigen Hilfsverb.

Can, must, may

2. Das unvollständige Hilfsverb *may*

Look at the following signs:

 You may turn right, but you may not turn left or go straight ahead.
Wenn das Verbot – wie hier – sehr streng ist, kannst du auch sagen:
You must not turn left!

 Auch *may* ist ein unvollständiges Hilfsverb und kann keine Vergangenheit bilden. Die Ersatzform kennst du bereits:

 You are allowed to turn right, but you are not allowed to turn left or to go straight ahead.

Exercise

D4 Write down what you may (not)/are (not) allowed to do when you see the following signs:

 1. You *may / are allowed to* use this door only in case of emergency.

2. You _____ enter the road.

 3. You _____ overtake cars, but you _____ overtake tractors.

4. You _____ bring your dog to the zoo, but you must keep it on the lead.

5. You _____ smoke here.

Can, must, may

Hier die Gegenwarts- und Vergangenheitsformen von *may* im Überblick:

		Ersatzform:
ich darf gehen	*I may go*	*I am/I'm allowed to go*
ich darf nicht gehen	*I may not go* *(I mustn't go)*	*I am/I'm not allowed to go*
ich durfte gehen	–	*I was allowed to go*
ich durfte nicht gehen	–	*I was not/wasn't allowed to go*

 D5 *In der folgenden Übung erzählt Fred von seiner ersten Klassenfahrt:*

What were Fred and his classmates allowed/not allowed to do?

We .... listen to music in our rooms or play cards in the evenings, but not longer than ten o'clock.

We .... make any noise after ten.

There was a little lake nearby, but

I .... go swimming there! We

.... go to the public swimming-bath – well, better than nothing!

They had quite a number of bicycles and go-carts, and we .... use them whenever we wanted. That was great fun!
On the last day my friend Chris wanted to go shopping to the town centre.

He .... to go alone, so I went with him.

Can, must, may

3. Das unvollständige Hilfsverb *must*

Instead of *must* you can use its substitute *have to*:

  Read Ann's answer aloud and use **have to**:

Well,
I **have to** help Granny this afternoon. ...
First I **have to** ...

 This is what Fred tells his mother after he has talked to Ann on the phone:

We can't play table-tennis today, because Ann's grandma is ill. Ann **has to** help her this afternoon. She **has to** ...

 In the evening Ann writes into her diary:

After school I couldn't play table-tennis with Fred. I **had to** help Granny all afternoon. But Fred came with me and gave me a hand. That was really nice of him! First we **had to** ...
...
When I came home I ...

Na, das klappt ja bestens! Es fehlt jetzt eigentlich nur noch die verneinte Form „etwas nicht tun müssen", dann birgt auch dieses unvollständige Hilfsverb keine Rätsel mehr. Aber jetzt heißt es:

Aufgepasst!
Am Wochenende muss ich nicht so früh aufstehen.
At weekends I   needn't   get up so early.
                don't have to

Hier darfst du dich nicht verleiten lassen, das deutsche Hilfsverb allzu wörtlich ins Englische zu übertragen, denn:

mustn't = nicht dürfen

Erinnerst du dich, in welchem Zusammenhang *mustn't* in diesem Kapitel schon einmal aufgetaucht ist? Genau – in Verbindung mit dem unvollständigen Hilfsverb *may*:

You *may not* turn left or go straight on.
You *mustn't* turn left or go straight on!

In der folgenden Übersicht sind die wichtigsten Formen zusammengefasst:

		Ersatzform:
ich muss gehen	*I must go*	*I have to go*
er muss gehen	*he must go*	*he has to go*
ich muss nicht gehen	*I needn't go*	*I don't have to go*
er muss nicht gehen	*he needn't go*	*he doesn't have to go*
ich musste gehen	–	*I had to go*
er musste gehen	–	*he had to go*
ich musste nicht gehen	–	*I didn't have to go*
er musste nicht gehen	–	*he didn't have to go*

Can, must, may

  In den Ferien muss man viele Dinge nicht tun, die sonst den Tagesablauf bestimmen. In der nächsten Übung träumt Nick gerade davon, was er in den Ferien nicht tun muss.

Holidays are great!

Nick thinks: In the holidays ...

I **don't have to** get up half past six.
I **don't have to** ...
...

You could also say:

I **needn't** get up at half past six.
I **needn't** ...
...

Now say what Nick **doesn't have to do** in the holidays:

He **doesn't have to** get up at half past six.
He **doesn't have to** ...

Can, must, may

D10 *Damit du* mustn't *und* needn't *(don't/doesn't have to) nicht so leicht verwechselst, hier noch eine Übung.*

Exercise

Fill in the correct **auxiliaries**:

You .... smoke too much.

I .... get up early tomorrow. There is no school.

You .... write Tom a letter, he will be here tomorrow.

But Margret, you .... hit your little brother!

Bob, you .... forget to answer Henry's letter.

Henry, you .... drink so much Coke.

You .... eat all that pudding if you are not hungry.

You .... forget to write to me soon.

You .... feed the dog, I've already done it.

Don't forget:
You needn't do that.	Du brauchst das nicht tun.
You don't have to do that.	Du musst das nicht tun.
You mustn't do that!	Du darfst das nicht tun!

Can, must, may

D11 In vielen Familien gibt es unerfreuliche Debatten, z. B. über die Frage, wer heute wieder mit dem Hund gehen oder wer das Geschirr abräumen soll. Kommt dir das irgendwie bekannt vor? Familie Sullivan hat dieses Problem auf ihre Weise gelöst: Für jede Woche gibt es einen „Dienstplan", in dem vermerkt ist, welche Aufgaben von wem zu erledigen sind:

	Mon	Tue	Wed	Thu	Fri	Sat	Sun
feed the rabbits + clean their cages	Paul	Paul	Paul	Paul	Paul	Paul	Paul
go for a walk with Scruffy (the dog)	Mum	Chris	Chris	Dad	Chris	Dad	Angie
water the flowers	Angie		Angie		Angie		Angie
lay the table	Dad + Chris						
clear the table	Angie + Paul						

Now say what Angie, Chris, Paul, Mr and Mrs Sullivan *had to do/didn't have to do* last week:

Example:

Last week Angie **had to** ...
She **didn't have to** ...
...

Chris **had to** ... on Tuesday, Wednesday and Friday
he **didn't have to** ...
Dad and Chris ...
...

Say what **you** had to do yesterday/last week!

Can, must, may

 D12 *Zum Abschluss kannst du jetzt überprüfen, ob du mit allen unvollständigen Hilfsverben bzw. ihren Ersatzformen zurechtkommst.*

At the zoo

There is a small zoo in our town. Last week I _____ (durfte) go there with my sister. My father _____ (konnte nicht) come with us, he _____ (musste) work, so we _____ (mussten) _____ take the bus. I _____ (durfte) take my brother's camera with me but I _____ (musste) promise him to be very careful.

When we reached the entrance we first _____ (mussten) buy the tickets. My sister _____ (durfte) visit the zoo for half the price, as she is only eight years old. First we went to the monkeys.

There was a sign: You _____ (dürfen nicht) feed the animals. The keeper told us that people who fed the monkeys _____ (mussten) _____ pay a high fine¹.   ¹ Geldstrafe

My sister likes the hippopotamus very much. She was very happy when she _____ (durfte) help the keeper to feed it. I _____ (musste) _____ take a picture of her in front of the pool.

We _____ (durften) ride on the elephant that carries visitors through the zoo. At six o'clock we _____ (mussten) leave the zoo.

4. Die unvollständigen Hilfsverben *can, must, may* und die Zukunft

So könnte Schüleraustausch im Jahr 2222 aussehen: Die beiden Jugendlichen vom Planeten Xenos befinden sich an Bord eines Raumschiffes, das eine Schülergruppe zur Erde bringt. Dort werden sie zwei Jahre lang zur Schule gehen und in Familien leben.

Die Zukunftsformen von *can*, *must* und *may* beherrschen die beiden Xenosianer schon recht gut. Und du?

  Ergänze die fehlenden Formen. Tipp: Schau dir die Sprechblasen noch einmal genau an!

Present		Future
they **can** understand	they **are able to** understand	they .... understand
they **can't** understand	they **are not able to** understand	they **will not (won't) be able to** understand
we **must** speak	we **have to** speak	we ....
we **needn't** speak	we **don't have to** ...	we ....
I **may** send	I **am allowed to** ...	I ....
I **may not/ mustn't** send	I **am not allowed to** ...	I ....

Can, must, may

 Xsi ist ein bisschen aufgeregt und macht sich viele Gedanken über den bevorstehenden Aufenthalt auf der Erde. Xias Vater war schon einmal als Austauschlehrer auf der Erde, und sie kann daher Xsis Fragen beantworten:

Fill in the **future tense forms**.

1. .... we .... (can) see Xenos from there?

2. No, you .... (cannot) see Xenos – it's too far away and it's too small. But there will be a video call every ten days, and you .... (can) see and talk to your family then.

3. Do you think we .... (must) stay inside the buildings all the time?

4. No, not at all. Earth kids like playing outside. When it rains or snows, we .... (must) wear special clothes.

5. .... we .... (must) go to school every day?

6. No. We .... (need not) go to school at the weekends, that is on Saturday and Sunday.

7. Is it true that we .... (may not) speak Xenophonic[1] at school?

8. That's right. We .... (must) speak Earthian[2] at school. But we .... (may) meet once a week and speak our own language then.

9. I've heard that they have a game called "baseball" on Earth. I hope I .... (can) play it – with all that gravitation[3] on Earth!

10. I'm sure you .... (may) join the school baseball team. And you will get used to gravitation within a short time.

[1] Xenophonic – hier: ausländisch, Sprache des Planeten Xenos
[2] Earthian – hier: Sprache der Erdbewohner
[3] Erdanziehung

Can, must, may

Test

Translate the following sentences:
Manchmal gibt es zwei Möglichkeiten, das Hilfsverb zu übersetzen.
(Je 2 Punkte für jeden richtigen Satz)

1. Als ich Windpocken hatte, durfte ich eine Woche lang nicht in die Schule gehen.

   When I had chickenpox, ...
   ....

2. Nächstes Jahr wird mein Bruder schwimmen können.

   ....

3. Ihr braucht/müsst nicht auf mich warten.

   ....

4. Ich konnte mit sechs Jahren noch nicht Fahrrad fahren.

   ....
   ....

5. Mr Brown wird zwei Stunden warten müssen. Der nächste Zug fährt um 10.20 Uhr.

   ....
   ....

   The next train leaves at 10.20 a. m.

[1] employees

6. In vielen Büros dürfen die Angestellten[1] nicht rauchen.

   ....
   ....

7. Jack muss heute auf seinen kleinen Bruder aufpassen.

   ....

8. Susan wird morgen nicht Volleyball spielen können. Sie hat sich den Knöchel verstaucht.

   ....
   ....

   She has sprained her ankle.

Can, must, may

Testauswertung

My personal scoreboard:

16–12 "right" scores:
This is an excellent result. You can be proud of yourself!

11–8 "right" scores:
Not bad! Analyse your mistakes and revise the forms you have problems with. Then you will soon be an expert in this field!

7–0 "right" scores:
You **can** do better than that! Are you sure you did **all** the exercises in this chapter? Well, then – work your way through this chapter again!

Word Power

Nie wieder sprachlos!
Don't be caught speechless!

Manchmal will man etwas auf Englisch ausdrücken, was auf Deutsch schon kompliziert klingt, und es fehlen einem buchstäblich die Worte. Unsere Devise lautet: *Don't be caught speechless!* oder *Where there's a will, there's a way!*

Oft ist es gar nicht nötig, etwas wörtlich ins Englische zu übersetzen. Es reicht, das Wesentliche inhaltlich wiederzugeben. Versuch's doch mal. – Erkläre Fred, was auf den Hinweisschildern steht:

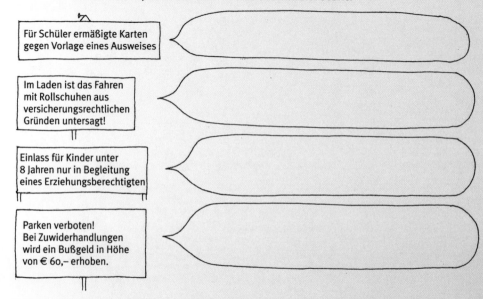

Manchmal fehlt dir in einer Unterhaltung oder beim Schreiben vielleicht nur ein bestimmtes Wort. Du willst es aber nicht einfach übergehen, weil es für deine Geschichte wichtig ist. Auch hier heißt es: flexibel sein! Du kannst das betreffende Wort so um- oder beschreiben, dass dein Gesprächspartner leicht darauf kommt, was du meinst.

Now it's your turn! Explain or describe the following things:

Schnorchel

Büroklammer

Spaten

Seestern

Kaulquappen

Schubkarre

Satellitenschüssel

Stabhochsprung

Die indirekte Rede
Reported speech

The Smiths are watching their favourite series on TV:

[1] Still! Pst!

In diesen Szenen eines Fernsehabends wird einiges gesprochen – sowohl auf dem Bildschirm als auch im Wohnzimmer der Smiths. In einer der Szenen wird das wiedergegeben, was eine andere Person vorher gesagt hat. Erinnerst du dich, welches Bild gemeint ist? – Granny hat wohl den Dialog zwischen Winston und Laura nicht ganz verstanden. In Bild 4 berichtet ihr Enkel, was genau gesagt wurde. Das bezeichnet man als **indirekte Rede** *(reported speech)*.

Indirekte Rede

E1 Lies die folgenden Sätze genau durch und trage sie in die richtige Spalte der Tabelle ein:

Oma sagte: „Ich habe mein Hörgerät verloren."
Granny said she had lost her hearing aid.
Granny said: "I've lost my hearing aid."
Oma sagte, sie habe ihr Hörgerät verloren.

	direct speech / wörtliche Rede	reported speech / indirekte Rede
englischer Satz		
deutscher Satz		

Bestimmt ist dir aufgefallen, dass in der **indirekten Rede** im Englischen **das Verb in einer anderen Zeit** steht als in der direkten Rede. Das liegt daran, dass in den Beispielen das **einleitende Verb** (*Granny said ...*) im *past tense* steht.

Whenever Mrs Jennings asks her daughter Helen to help her with the housework, Helen *says* that she *has* to do a lot of homework.

> **Regel**: Steht das **einleitende Verb in der Gegenwart, ändert sich die Zeit** in der indirekten Rede **nicht**.

Da diese Fälle meist keine Schwierigkeiten bereiten, wollen wir uns hier nicht weiter mit ihnen beschäftigen.
Aber auch die Veränderung der Zeiten in den Sätzen, in denen das einleitende Verb in der Vergangenheit steht, ist eigentlich ganz einfach. Es gibt dafür feste Regeln. Wenn du sie beachtest, kannst du kaum etwas falsch machen.

Indirekte Rede

1. Die Zeitenfolge in der indirekten Rede

This is what the presidential candidate said in his speech:

This country needs a man of experience, a man who keeps his promises. In the past huge sums of money were wasted. I have often criticised this in public. I will not spend millions on …

In his speech at a party meeting last night the Republican candidate said that this country needed a man of experience, a man who kept his promises. He went on to say that in the past huge sums of money had been wasted, and that he had often criticised that in public. He told his audience that he would not spend millions on …

  Ergänze das folgende Schaubild. Dann wirst du ganz leicht erkennen, wie sich die Zeiten in der indirekten Rede verändern.

	direct speech	reported speech
Verb Tense	needs simple present	needed simple past
Verb Tense	keeps 	
Verb Tense	were wasted simple past	
Verb Tense	have criticised present perfect	

An einem Zeitstrahl lässt sich die Zeitverschiebung gut darstellen:

past perfect	simple past	present perfect	simple present
he had kept	he kept	he has kept	he keeps

Indirekte Rede

> Steht das **einleitende Verb** in der **Vergangenheit,** ändert sich die Zeit bei der Umwandlung von wörtlicher in indirekte Rede wie folgt:
>
> | | | |
> |---|---|---|
> | present tense | → | past tense |
> | present perfect | → | past perfect |
> | past tense | → | past perfect |
> | past perfect | bleibt | past perfect |

Regel

Und was wird aus dem Futur?
Schauen wir uns noch einmal den letzten Satz der Rede an, die der ehrgeizige Präsidentschaftskandidat gehalten hat.

Er sagte: "*I will not spend millions on ...*"

Aus dem Munde der Nachrichtensprecherin klang das so:

He said that he would not spend millions on ...

Ergänzen wir also die oben aufgeführte Regel:

> | | | |
> |---|---|---|
> | future I | → | conditional I |
> | (will + Verb) | | (would + Verb) |

Regel

Indirekte Rede

 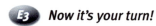 **Now it's your turn!**

Bad luck

John wanted to go to Sarah's birthday party, but he's in hospital now. His mother rings up Sarah and tells her what happened:

 John is very sorry that he can't come to your party. He has been taken to hospital. There was a football match at the school this morning. It was the final of the school championship. John was just running to get the ball when he slipped, fell and broke his ankle. Fortunately, his leg doesn't hurt too badly. He will stay in hospital for two days and he won't be able to go to school for at least a week.

In the afternoon Sarah tells her friends:

John's mother rang me up an hour ago. She said he _was_

very sorry that he _____ to the party. She told me

(that) he _____ to hospital. There _____

a football match at the school this morning. It _____

the final of the school championship. She said (that) John _____

_____ to get the ball when he _____

_____ his ankle. Fortunately, his leg _____

_____ too badly. She also said he _____ in

hospital for two days and he _____ to go to school
for at least a week.

In einigen Sätzen der vorangegangenen Übung war ein Wort eingeklammert, das man einfügen oder auch weglassen kann: *that* (dass).

His mother told me that he had been taken to hospital.
   Seine Mutter sagte mir, dass er ins Krankenhaus gebracht worden sei.
His mother told me he had been taken to hospital.
   Seine Mutter sagte mir, er sei ins Krankenhaus gebracht worden.

Du kannst von Fall zu Fall entscheiden, ob du die Version mit oder ohne *that* bevorzugst.

E4 *Decide whether or not to use* that *in the next exercise.*

The Bushfire

Sandy Smith often reads to her grandma. As Granny doesn't hear very well, Sandra sometimes has to repeat sentences. She uses indirect speech then.

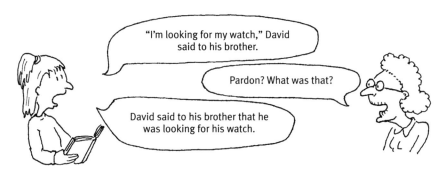

Repeat the following sentences in indirect speech:

1. He said: "I had a fight with a kangaroo."

   ....

2. David told Steve: "The birds are flying north."

   ....

3. The man behind the desk said to David: "I've tried to phone you at least ten times."

   ....
   ....

4. Helen said: "I'm sure that the two men will be found."

   ....
   ....

5. Jim said to the fireman: "I need a helmet and an axe."

   ....

6. He added: "Something has to be done!"

   ....

7. The reporter said: "Nobody was killed in the fire."

   ....

2. Weitere Veränderungen in der indirekten Rede

Häufig verändert sich in der indirekten Rede nicht nur die Zeitform des Verbs.

Friday, 10 a. m.   Friday, 6 p. m.   Sunday, 3 p. m.

Du siehst, auch Pronomen und Zeitangaben werden verändert:

> we   ⟶   they
> tomorrow   ⟶   the next day
>
> Die **Veränderung** ist **abhängig** davon, **von wem, wo** und **wann** das **Gesagte wiedergegeben** wird.

Hier eine Liste der häufigsten Veränderungen:

Zeitangaben

today	that day
tonight	that night
this morning/afternoon	that morning/afternoon
yesterday	the day before
	the previous day
tomorrow	the next day
	the following day
now	then, at that point
next week/month/year	the following week/month/year
last week	the previous week
	the week before
an hour/a week ago	an hour/a week before

Ortsangaben

here	there, in that place
in this street	in that street

Indirekte Rede

 Alles klar? Dann versuch's mal mit der folgenden Übung:

Paul's friend Tony and his family have moved to another town. One day Paul visits them there. This is what Tony tells him:

① There are no kids in our neighbourhood here.

② My new school is more than five miles away.

③ My new classmates are really nice. Some of them asked me to join the football team.

④ Tomorrow I'm going to a school party.

⑤ Yesterday I was at the sports centre. It's great! I've never seen anything like this before!

A few days later Paul tells his friends at home:

1. Last week I visited Tony and his family. Tony said

2. He explained to me that

3. And he said

4. Then he told me

5. He also told me

Indirekte Rede

3. Fragen in der indirekten Rede

Vor dem Supermarkt, in dem auch Fred oft einkauft, wird eine Umfrage durchgeführt.

1. *How old are you?*
2. *Why did you come here?*
3. *How often do you come here?*
4. *How long have you been here?*
5. *Do you buy all your things here?*
6. *Do you have a car?*
7. *Do you park your car in the supermarket car park?*

The next day Fred tells his friend Ron:

[2] eine Umfrage durchführen

"At the supermarket they carried out a survey [2].
A young man interviewed Mrs Moore.

1. *First he wanted to know how old she was.*
2. *Then he asked her why she had gone there.*
3. *Then he asked her how often she went there.*
4. *And he asked how long she had been there.*
5. *He wanted to know if she bought all her things there.*
6. *He also wanted to know if she had a car and*
7. *whether she parked her car in the supermarket car park."*

 Auch bei indirekten Fragesätzen verändert sich die Zeitform des Verbs in der indirekten Rede nur, wenn das **einleitende Verb in der Vergangenheit** steht.

Betrachten wir nun die Satzstellung in der wörtlichen beziehungsweise in der indirekten Rede etwas genauer. Bei den Fragen haben wir es mit zwei verschiedenen Arten zu tun:

– mit Entscheidungsfragen *(yes/no questions):*

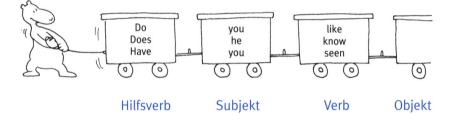

84

Indirekte Rede

– oder mit Fragen, die durch ein Fragewort eingeleitet werden:

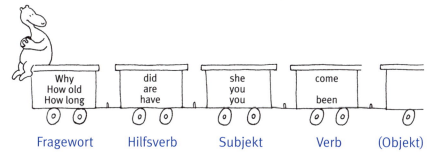

In der indirekten Rede sehen die Fragen dann so aus:

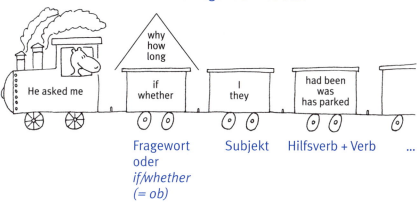

> Die **Fragewörter** der wörtlichen Rede tauchen auch in der indirekten Rede wieder auf:

How old …?	… wanted to know	how old …
Why …?		why …
How often …?	… asked me	how often …
How long …?		how long …

Entscheidungsfragen

beginnen in der wörtlichen Rede mit einem Hilfsverb:	In der indirekten Rede werden sie mit *if* bzw. *whether* eingeleitet:		
Did you buy …?	… asked me	if/whether	I had bought …
Do you like …?			I liked …
Have you seen …?	… wanted to know	if/whether	I had seen …
Can you swim?			I could swim.

> Beachte, dass in indirekten Fragen das Subjekt vor dem Hilfsverb bzw. Verb steht (wie in Aussagesätzen)!
> Die Umschreibung mit *do/does/did* entfällt im indirekten Fragesatz!

Indirekte Rede

Hier noch einmal die wichtigsten Regeln in Kurzform:

> **Indirekte Fragesätze** (einleitendes Verb in der Vergangenheit):
> - Zeitenfolge beachten
> - Umschreibung mit *do* entfällt
> - Fragewörter bleiben
> - bei Entscheidungsfragen *if* (oder *whether*) verwenden
> - **Subjekt** steht **vor** dem (Hilfsverb +) Verb

 Now it's your turn.
The pupils in Linda's class are working on a project called "Teenagers and television". This is an extract from the questionnaire[1] they have put together:

[1] Fragebogen

1. How many hours per day do you spend in front of the "box"[2]?
2. What did you watch yesterday? Which programmes? How long?
3. Are there any programmes you watch regularly?
4. Do you never/sometimes/often switch channels in the middle of a programme?
5. How many TV sets are there in your flat/house?
6. Have you got a TV set of your own?
7. Have you ever switched off the telly[3] because you didn't like the film/programme?   ❏ Never.   ❏ Once or twice.   ❏ Often.
8. What do you do during commercial breaks?

[2] Kurzform von goggle box = die „Glotze"

[3] telly = television

Joe writes a report for the school magazine. (Complete the sentences!)

1. The first thing we wanted to know was how many hours per day the pupils ………………………………………… in front of the "box".

2. We asked them ………………………………………………

3. and ………………………………………………………………

4. We also wanted to find out ……………………………………
   ………………………………………………………………………

5. Of course we asked ……………………………………………
   ………………………………………………………………………

6. and ………………………………………………………………

Indirekte Rede

7. Apart from that we wanted to know ....

....

8. and ....

Und wie sehen deine Fernsehgewohnheiten aus? – Why don't **you** answer the questions of the questionnaire?! Say what kinds of programmes you often/sometimes/never watch etc.!

Here is some vocabulary that might be useful:

Wortliste

sports (programme)	Sport(sendung)
news (programme)	Nachrichten(sendung)
documentary	Reportage, Bericht
situation comedy	lustige Familiensendung
series, serial	Serie
detective film	Krimi
music programme	Musiksendung
game show	Spielshow
movie	Spielfilm

E7 A star is born

Exercise

Daisy Doolittle wants to become a famous film star. She has an interview with a producer who asks her a lot of questions:

1. Can you sing?
2. In which plays have you already acted?
3. Are you interested in a role in advertising?
4. Do you like cats?

Later that day she tells her friend Jane about the interview. Complete what Daisy says:

1. The procucer wanted to know ....

2. He asked me ....

3. Then he wanted to know ....

4. At the end of the interview he asked me ....

....

By the way – Daisy got the role!

4. Befehlssätze in der indirekten Rede

In the studio the director and his assistant tell Daisy what to do:

In the evening Daisy talks to her friend Jane again:

Die wörtlichen Befehlssätze beginnen jeweils mit einem Imperativ:

Move to the right ...
Don't speak ...

Indirekte Rede

> Der indirekte Befehlssatz wird mit einem Verb des Befehlens eingeleitet. Danach steht die Person, der der Befehl gegeben wurde, und der Infinitiv des Verbs:

... asked	me	to sing ...	... bat mich ... zu singen
... told	me	not to walk ...	... sagte mir, ich solle nicht ...
... wanted	me	to move ...	... wollte, dass ich ... gehe.
... ordered	me	not to speak ...	... gab mir die Anweisung/befahl mir, nicht ... zu sprechen.

> Es spielt hier keine Rolle, in welcher Zeit das einleitende Verb steht. – Der indirekte Befehlssatz sieht immer gleich aus:

My mum always tells me to eat slowly .
  Meine Mutter sagt mir immer, ich solle langsam essen.

My mum told me to eat slowly .
  Meine Mutter sagte mir, ich solle langsam essen.

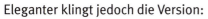

Natürlich kann man einen indirekten Befehlssatz auch umständlicher mit *should* bilden:

My dad said that I should switch off the TV.

Eleganter klingt jedoch die Version:

My dad told me to switch off the TV.

Indirekte Rede

Exercise E8 — It's time for an exercise!

Sally is waiting for her friend. Finally Ann arrives – but she is 45 minutes late!

1. First, Tim wanted me ....
....

2. Then Grandma asked me ....
....

3. The worst thing was that Mum ordered me ....
....

4. Then Andy came in and ....
....

5. When I said goodbye, Dad ....
....

Exercise E9 — The next day Sally's mother asked why Ann had been so late the day before. Sally said:

"Well, first Tim wanted her to help him with his maths homework. Then her grandmother ....

....

....

....

....

....

Indirekte Rede

Test

1. Europe in seven days

(Je 1 Punkt für jede Verbform und für jeden Ausdruck, der sich in der indirekten Rede verändert – maximal 14 Punkte)

Mr Running from San Francisco is "doing" Europe in seven days. From Paris he rings up his wife. Here is what he tells her:

"I'm ringing you up from Paris. It's a beautiful city. I've already seen the Eiffel Tower. Yesterday we went to Versailles, that famous castle where the French kings had lived. There is gold everywhere, but I didn't see any bathrooms! Tomorrow I will be in Rome. A bus will take us to the most interesting sights. I've already taken hundreds of photos. Well, I must go! We are meeting at the Louvre at two o'clock."

Two days later Mrs Running meets her neighbour. She tells her about the phone call:

"Yes, he called me the day before yesterday. He said he .... from Paris and it .... a beautiful city. He told me that he .... the Eiffel Tower. .... they .... to Versailles, that famous castle where the French kings .... Rupert said that there .... gold everywhere, but he .... any bathrooms! He then explained to me that he .... in Rome .... A bus .... them to the most interesting sights. The last thing he said was that he .... hundreds of photos and that he .... to go because they .... at the Louvre at two o'clock."

91

Indirekte Rede

2. Übertrage die folgenden Sätze in die indirekte Rede:

Manchmal musst du ein anderes einleitendes Verb verwenden.
(Je 2 Punkte für jeden richtigen Satz)

a Shirley asked her friend: "Do you like my dress?"

．．．

b The teacher told Mary: "Please repeat the sentence!"

．．．

c The gangster shouted to the old lady: "Give me your handbag!"

．．．

d The policeman asked the visitor: "Where did you see the man?"

．．．

e Lisa's new classmates wanted to know: "Have you already been to the school cafeteria?"

．．．

f Mrs Scott said to her little son: "Don't throw the peas on the floor!"

．．．

Indirekte Rede

Testauswertung

My personal scoreboard:

26–20 "right" scores:
Excellent! You couldn't have done better!

19–12 "right" scores:
That's really good for a start! You just need a little more practice. Revise the tenses (chapter A in this book) or the aspects of the reported speech you had problems with.

11–0 "right" scores:
Are you sure you read the whole chapter and did all the exercises? You will see: practice makes perfect!

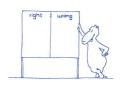

Word Power

Nachschlagen im Wörterbuch II
How to use the dictionary II

In order to understand the important passages of a story, it is sometimes helpful to look up some words in the dictionary. For Christoph, who is just reading an exciting criminal story, it would make things a lot clearer:

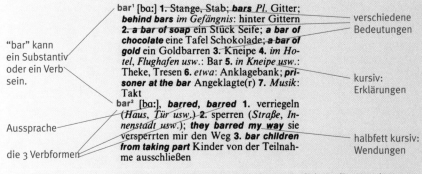

aus: Langenscheidts Power Dictionary English, Berlin, München 2004

Now let's have a look at the different meanings of the English word *bar*. Write down the German translation of bar in the sentence Christoph has just read:

The gangsters were put behind bars. ....

Now do the same, only with different words. What do they mean?

He was **engaged** as a foreman.

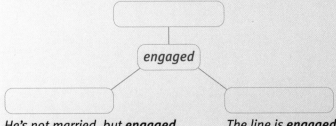

He's not married, but **engaged**.   The line is **engaged**.

She was **moved** to tears.

move

They **moved** to Munich.

Don't **move**!

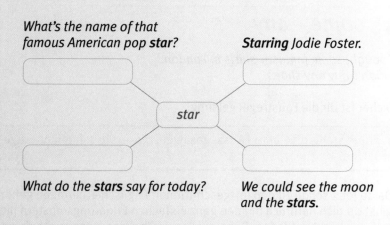

What's the name of that famous American pop **star**?

Starring Jodie Foster.

star

What do the **stars** say for today?

We could see the moon and the **stars**.

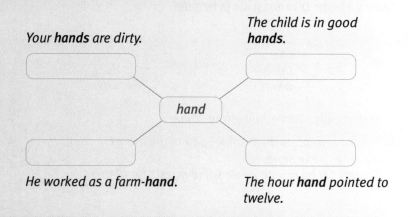

Your **hands** are dirty.

The child is in good **hands**.

hand

He worked as a farm-**hand**.

The hour **hand** pointed to twelve.

Some – any, much – many:
Unbestimmte Pronomen
Indefinite pronouns

1. *some – any*

I bought some fantastic shirts in London.
I didn't buy any shoes.

Sicher ist dir die Faustregel geläufig:

> *Some* steht in bejahten Aussagesätzen, *any* in verneinten Aussagesätzen.

Da du jetzt schon zu den fortgeschrittenen EnglischlernerInnen gehörst, gibst du dich natürlich mit den ganz einfachen Erklärungsmustern nicht mehr so leicht zufrieden. Daher wollen wir in diesem Abschnitt einige Ergänzungen anfügen, um das Bild von *some* und *any* abzurunden.

Alles, was du jetzt liest, gilt übrigens für alle Zusammensetzungen mit *some* und *any*. Du kennst sie ja bereits:

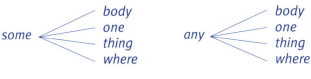

Zunächst einige Anmerkungen zu *some*:

a) *I heard a noise. Is there somebody in the room?*
b) *Would you like some tea?*
   Wouldn't it be nice to invite some guests for dinner?

Some verwendest du
a) in **Fragesätzen**, wenn du als **Antwort „ja"** erwartest,
b) in **Fragesätzen**, die eine **Bitte**, eine **Einladung** oder ein **Angebot** darstellen.

Unbestimmte Pronomen

Weiter mit *any*:

Is there any soup left?
Aren't there any glasses in the cupboard?

> Du verwendest *any* in **Fragesätzen**, wenn du **nicht sicher** bist, ob die Antwort „Ja" oder „Nein" lauten wird.

Regel

You can call me at any time.	jederzeit; egal, zu welcher Zeit
I want to go anywhere as long as it is warm.	wo immer; egal, wohin
Do your homework first. After that you can do anything you like!	alles; egal was

> Du kannst *any* auch in bejahten Sätzen verwenden. Es bezeichnet dann eine **beliebige Sache** oder **Person**.
>
> *anybody*   irgendjemand (egal, wer)
> *anything*   alles (egal, was)
> *anywhere*   überall (egal, wo/wohin)

Regel

Nun zu unserem Übungsteil:

 F1   Kreuze das richtige Wort an und ergänze die Sätze. Manchmal gibt es auch zwei Möglichkeiten!   *Exercise*

	some	somebody someone	something	somewhere
There is _____ in the car.				
Give me _____ apples, please.				
The camera must be _____.				
I want _____ to drink.				
There are _____ sausages left.				
_____ is behind you.				
Let's meet _____ else.				
I've just bought _____ cheese.				
_____ is wrong with my watch.				

Unbestimmte Pronomen

	any	anybody anyone	any-thing	any-where
I don't know .... here.				
Is there .... money left?				
Has .... got a hanky¹?				
Have you seen him .... ?				
Is .... wrong?				
I haven't got .... sugar.				
That doesn't make .... sense.				
.... else?				
I haven't got .... friends.				

¹ ugs. Taschentuch

Exercise

F2 *In der nächsten Übung kommen* some *und* any *(somebody, anybody, ...) vermischt vor. Setze die richtige Form ein.*

1. The box is empty. There isn't .... in it.
2. There are .... pencils on the writing-desk.
3. I need .... to help me with the washing-up.
4. You can phone me at .... time.
5. Why don't we go .... else?
6. Can you see my purse .... ?
7. Would you like .... sandwiches?

Wortliste

Anstelle von *not ... any* kann man auch *no...* sagen:

not any   = *no*
not anything   = *nothing*
not anybody   = *nobody, no one*
not anywhere   = *nowhere*

Unbestimmte Pronomen

 Sieh dir den folgenden Beispielsatz an und wandle dann die vorgegebenen Sätze entsprechend um:

1. There's nothing in it. — There isn't anything in it.
2. We can see it nowhere.
3. There are no stamps on the letter.
4. Nobody was in the room.
5. He does nothing all day.

2. each – every

"Fred goes jogging every day."

Fred has got an aquarium in his room. Each fish has got a name.

every	each
bezeichnet jede(n), jedes allgemein bzw. jede(n), jedes ohne Ausnahme.	heißt es, wenn es sich um eine begrenzte Anzahl handelt und jede(r), jedes Einzelne aus dieser Gruppe gemeint ist.

Regel

Some more examples:

Every house has got a roof.

Every child likes ice-cream.

I think *everybody* knows "Jingle Bells".

Each pupil in the class …

There are fifteen houses in this street.

Each door is painted in a different colour.

Unbestimmte Pronomen

Exercise *What's the name of the game?*

Fill in *each* or *every*:

_____ (1) child in the U. S. A. knows this game.

To play it, you need two teams. _____ (2) team has nine players. The game is played on a large field. One player throws a ball, another player tries to hit it with a long wooden stick. In order to make a "run" a player must touch _____ (3) of the four "bases".

Almost _____ (4) American high school has a ? team.

3. much – many – a lot (of)

"And the weather forecast said there wouldn't be much rain today!"

There weren't many people in the stadium.

Regel

| Much (viel) verwendet man bei nicht zählbaren Substantiven. | Many (viele) verwendet man bei zählbaren Substantiven. |

Fred has got a lot of CDs.

When it's hot Fred drinks a lot of water.

Regel

A lot of (oder etwas umgangssprachlicher: *lots of*) kann man sowohl bei zählbaren als auch bei nicht zählbaren Substantiven verwenden.

Sandra spends *a lot of money* on clothes.

There hasn't been *a lot of sunshine* lately.
There hasn't been *much sunshine* lately.

Did you get *a lot of Valentine cards*?
Did you get *many Valentine cards*?

> In der Regel stehen *much* und *many* nur in **Fragesätzen und verneinten Sätzen**.
> *a lot of (lots of)* steht in **bejahten und verneinten Aussagesätzen sowie in Fragesätzen**.

Regel

 Fill in much, many *or* a lot of:

Exercise

Jane's mother: What was the concert like? Were there .... (1) people?

Jane: Well, I met David, Linda and Michael in front of the concert hall. We were rather early, so at first there weren't .... (2) people. But after a while it got really crowded. I saw quite .... (3) boys and girls from my school. When the band came onto the stage, ... (4) fans moved forward, so there wasn't .... (5) space left. But the show was fantastic. They played .... (6) really good songs.

4. (a) little – (a) few

We had dinner in *a nice little Italian restaurant*.	... in einem netten kleinen italienischen Restaurant
Could I have *a little milk*, please?	... etwas/ein bisschen/ein wenig ...
They had *little hope* of winning the match.	... wenig ...

little vor einem **zählbaren Substantiv** (house, cup, child) bedeutet:	klein
a little vor **nicht zählbaren Substantiven** (sugar, fun, water) heißt:	etwas, ein bisschen
little vor einem **nicht zählbaren Substantiv** bedeutet:	wenig

Regel

Unbestimmte Pronomen

I've got *a few pounds* left. ... ein paar ...
Few people know that he's a millionaire. ... wenige ...

a few steht **nur vor zählbaren Substantiven:**	ein paar, einige
few steht ebenfalls **nur vor zählbaren Substantiven:**	wenige

few und *little* klingen oft etwas förmlich und können durch andere Ausdrücke ersetzt werden:

statt *few*: not many, hardly any
statt *little*: not much, hardly any

 F6 Auch hierzu eine kleine Übung:

A weekend trip

Fill in *(a) few* or *(a) little*:

My brother likes old castles, so we visited one at the weekend. I only know very .... (1) about castle architecture, but my brother explained everything to us! There were only .... (2) people around, so we could go wherever we liked. From the tower (236 steps to the top!) we had a wonderful view and we saw that there was .... (3) lake nearby. I was .... (4) tired after climbing up that tower. I said to the others that I would like to go down to the lake. Mum had made .... (5) sandwiches and she had also packed some apples and a bottle of orange juice into .... (6) basket. So we had a picnic by the lake.

Test

Für den Abschlusstest haben wir *some, any, each, every, much, many, a lot of, (a) few* and *(a) little* noch einmal gut durchgemischt. – Es ist angerichtet:

(Je 1 Punkt für jeden richtigen Ausdruck)

1. Hast du heute Nachmittag viel zu tun?

   Have you got .... work to do this afternoon?

Unbestimmte Pronomen

2. Es tut mir leid, ich habe keine Cola. Aber es ist etwas Milch im Kühlschrank. Wie wär's damit?

   I'm sorry, I haven't got .... coke. But there is .... milk in the fridge. How about that?

3. Gloria und Juliet gehen jeden Samstag zusammen zum Joggen.

   Gloria and Juliet go jogging together .... Saturday.

4. Möchtest du noch etwas Tee?

   Would you like .... more tea?

5. Verzeihung, wie komme ich bitte zum British Museum?
   – Sie können jeden beliebigen Bus von dieser Haltestelle aus nehmen.

   Excuse me, how can I get to the British Museum, please?

   – You can take .... bus from this stop.

6. Ms Redgrave hat fünf Katzen. Jede ihrer Katzen hat ein eigenes Körbchen.

   Ms Redgrave has five cats. .... of her cats has a basket of its own.

7. Wir hatten nicht viel Zeit, deshalb schrieben wir nur ein paar Postkarten.

   We didn't have .... time, so we only wrote .... postcards.

8. Ich war ein bisschen überrascht, als ich hörte, dass Rick die Fußballmannschaft verlassen hatte.

   I was .... surprised when I heard that Rick had left the football team.

Testauswertung

My personal scoreboard:

10–8 "right" scores:
Very good – you can be proud of yourself!

7–6 "right" scores:
Not too bad! Revise the indefinite pronouns that you got wrong.

5–0 "right" scores:
Have another look at the examples and exercises in this chapter. Then you will do better next time!

Word Power

Lesen
Reading

Reading is good for your English! In fact, English is everywhere around you – just keep your eyes open. You will find English texts on/in:

tins or packages

instructions

stage readers

English magazines

[1] besser werden

Try to read English texts regularly. Even if you just read them for the fun of it and even if you don't look up every single word, your English will improve[1]. We would like to show you that you do not always have to look up a word in the dictionary in order to understand its meaning. And that makes reading a lot easier than you may have thought.

"Old Master" turned out to be a forgery

At a press conference held earlier this week the manager of a famous London art gallery announced that one of the old paintings that were to be sold to a rich American art collector was a forgery. A very good forgery, even experts had to admit! Nobody would ever have found out if the collector from Boston had not seen the original at a friend's house some weeks before. Then exactly the same painting was offered to him in London.

Chemical tests proved that the art gallery only had a copy, and not the "Old Master". Specialists at Scotland Yard are now investigating the matter. Several people working at the gallery have been questioned so far. Quite a number of private collectors as well as museums pay extra sums for expensive chemical tests to find out whether they, too, have a "Fake Master" on their wall!

Can cou guess what the words mean?

| collector | .... | investigate | .... |
| forgery | .... | chemical | .... |

How can you find out the meaning of a word?

The following check-list might help you:

1. Do I know a word from the same word family?
   Fill in the missing words:

collector	collect	fame	....
painting	paint	follower	....
knowledge	....	changeable	....
meaningful	....	talkative	....

2. Is there a similar word in German?

chemical	chemisch	shoulder blade	....
information	Information	politician	....
decoration	....	repair	....
organize	....	mass media	....

3. Can I guess the meaning from the context?

   "Old Master" turned out to be a forgery.

   ... the manager of a famous London art gallery announced that one of the old paintings that were to be sold to a rich American art collector was a forgery.

   Well, you may not know what forgery means when reading the headline.

   But from the context of the article it becomes quite clear that forgery means "Fälschung"!

You see – you don't have to look up every word you don't know. A bit of intelligent guessing can make life a lot easier!

Das Passiv
The passive

At a building site

[1] Baustelle

In the street where Fred lives there's a building site[1].

Exercise G1 *Which of the following statements are true, which are false?*

	true	false
1. When Fred came to the site this morning three walls had already been finished.	☐	☐
2. The cement was brought by a big cement mixer truck.	☐	☐
3. Most of the windows have already been put in.	☐	☐
4. Tomorrow the house will be finished.	☐	☐
5. Heavy parts are lifted by a crane.	☐	☐

Exercise G2 *Um welche Zeiten handelt es sich bei den Sätzen aus Exercise 1? Wenn dir die Namen der Zeiten nicht mehr geläufig sind, kannst du sie in Kapitel A nachlesen.*

1. ... three walls **had already been built**.   past perfect

2. The cement **was brought** ...   .

3. ... the windows **have already been put** in.   ....

4. ... the house **will be finished**.   ....

5. Heavy parts **are lifted** ...   .

1. Die Zeitformen des Passivs

Hier siehst du eine Übersicht. Das Passiv wird immer mit einer Form des Verbs *(to) be* und dem *Past Participle* gebildet.

Subjekt	Form des Verbs *(to) be*	past participle	
The wall	is	built ...	
The walls	are	built ...	*present tense*
The wall	was	built ...	
The walls	were	built ...	*past tense*
The wall	has been	built ...	
The walls	have been	built ...	*present perfect*
The wall(s)	had been	built ...	*past perfect*
The wall(s)	will be	built ...	*future*

In den folgenden Übungen kannst du das Passiv in verschiedenen Zeiten üben. Fangen wir mit der Gegenwart an.

 Let's have a look at a garage. What is done here?

Exercise

Übrigens:
Wenn du Vokabeln rund ums Auto wiederholen möchtest, wirf doch mal einen Blick auf die **Word power**-Seiten 18/19.
Hier eine kleine Auswahl:

engine	*Motor*	plugs	*Zündkerzen*
tyres	*Reifen*	windscreen	
brakes	*Bremsen*	wipers	*Scheibenwischer*

 1. engines/repair   Engines are repaired.

 2. tyres/pump up

Passiv

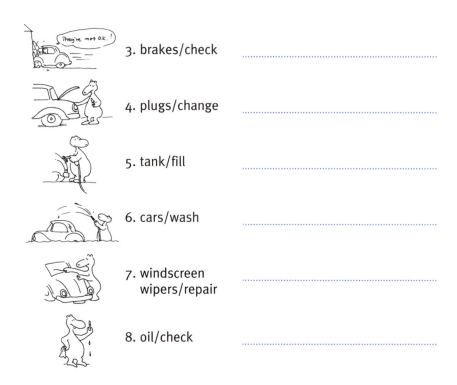

3. brakes/check ....

4. plugs/change ....

5. tank/fill ....

6. cars/wash ....

7. windscreen wipers/repair ....

8. oil/check ....

Da diese Arbeiten in einer Werkstatt Tag für Tag erledigt werden, steht hier immer *simple present*.
Wenn wir uns jedoch eine ganz bestimmte Szene ansehen, die sich gerade im Moment abspielt, muss auch im Passiv die *progressive form* stehen.

Was passiert gerade in der folgenden Szene?

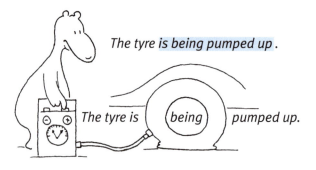

The tyre is being pumped up.

The tyre is (being) pumped up.

Regel

Schiebe *being* zwischen am/is/are / was/were und *past participle* – und schon hast du die Verlaufsform des Passivs!
Die Verlaufsform des Passivs kommt nur im *present tense* und im *past tense* vor.

Passiv

G4 What is being done in the following picture?

1. The tyres ....
2. The car ....
3. The radio ....
4. The oil ....
5. The lights ....

> And here is another good tip:
> Whenever you come across a picture (e. g. in a magazine), why don't you name the things that are being done?!

Tipp

G5 In der nächsten Übung geht es um die Vergangenheit.

Florida was hit hardest by hurricane "Bonny". Hundreds of houses **were damaged**. It seems like a miracle that nobody **was killed**.

Fill in the correct passive forms of the verbs in brackets.

1. 52 persons *(injure)* ....
2. A bus *(sweep)* [1] .... off the road.
3. Cars *(overturn)* ....
4. Trees *(uproot)* [2] ....
5. A bridge *(destroy)* ....
6. The fire department *(call)* ....
   twenty-seven times last night.

[1] (to) sweep-swept-swept: fegen

[2] entwurzeln

109

Passiv

Exercise G6 A burglary

Mr and Mrs Townsend have just come home from the theatre. When they enter their living room they are shocked. There has been a burglary. They call the police immediately. One of the policemen makes some notes.

Complete the sentences.

1. The living room window *(break)* has been broken.
2. The wardrobe *(open)* _____.
3. All the clothes *(throw)* _____ on the floor.
4. Papers *(tear)* _____ to pieces.
5. The TV set *(smash up)* _____.
6. The silver candle sticks *(take away)* _____.
7. The stamp collection *(steal)* _____.
8. A bottle of whisky *(drink)* _____.
9. The radio *(damage)* _____.

Exercise G7 A few days after the burglary Mr and Mrs Townsend are talking to their neighbour: "We came home from the theatre at about eleven o'clock. When we entered the living room we both couldn't believe what we saw –

The window had been broken.
The wardrobe …"

Go on. Look at the sentences above and use the *past perfect* this time.

Eine Übung zum Futur findest du an späterer Stelle in diesem Kapitel. Jetzt geht es zunächst weiter mit der Frage: Wie unterscheiden sich die Formen von Aktiv und Passiv?

2. Aktiv und Passiv

Das Verb *(to) be* spielt sowohl bei der Bildung von Aktiv- als auch von Passiv-Formen eine wichtige Rolle. Auf den ersten Blick scheint es schwierig, all die verschiedenen Möglichkeiten auseinanderzuhalten. Aber du wirst sehen – Übung schafft den Durchblick!

Du hast das Verb *(to) be* bisher verwendet

als **Vollverb**:

This is my pen.	ist
Here are your books.	sind
They were in London.	waren

als Teil der *progressive form*:

Fred is making a pancake.	macht gerade
Ann was playing tennis.	spielte gerade

Nun kommt das **Passiv** hinzu:

Fred is often asked …	wird oft gefragt
The windows were shut.	wurden geschlossen
The car will be sold.	wird verkauft werden

Passiv

  In dieser Übung sollst du nun feststellen,
- ob es sich um Aktiv oder Passiv handelt und
- in welcher Zeit die Sätze stehen.

	active/passive	tense
Tom is writing a letter.	active	present
This machine was built in the USA.		
This parcel has been opened before.		
My friend has often been in London.		
These recorders are made in Japan.		
We are making a doll.		
The car was stolen last night.		
They were very happy.		
The books were read by many people.		
Your father will be very angry.		
A new hotel will be built in our street.		

Oft kann man einen Aktiv-Satz in eine Passiv-Konstruktion umformen – und umgekehrt. Hier ein Beispiel:

Aktiv:
A famous pop star will sing the national anthem.

Passiv:
The national anthem will be sung by a famous pop star.
(von ...)

Aus dem **Akkusativobjekt des Aktivsatzes** (wen oder was?) **wird** das **Subjekt des Passivsatzes** (wer oder was?).

Aus dem Subjekt des Aktivsatzes *(A famous pop star)* wird im Passivsatz: **by** *a famous pop star.*

Passiv

 Change the following sentences from the active into the passive voice. Use the same tense as in the given sentence.

1. A lot of newspaper editors printed President Bush's speech.

   President Clinton's speech was printed by a lot of newspaper editors.

2. Thousands of people visit Ailwee Cave every summer.

   ....

3. The magician cut Fred in two.

   ....

4. Four waiters had brought in the wedding cake.

   ....

5. More than 200,000 people have already bought the new Madonna CD.

   ....

6. The French team won the World Cup last year.

   ....

7. The mayor will open the exhibition next Friday.

   ....

3. Das Passiv in Verbindung mit *can*, *must* und *may*

Sehen wir uns noch einmal auf der Baustelle in der Nähe von Freds Zuhause um:

At the building site helmets **must be worn** by everybody.

> In Verbindung mit *can*, *must* und *may* wird das Passiv mit *be* und der 3. Form des Verbs gebildet.

Lots of things	*can be seen* ...
	... können gesehen werden
Helmets	*must be worn* ...
	... müssen getragen werden
Photos	*may be taken* ...
	... dürfen gemacht werden
Rubbish	*mustn't be thrown* ...
	... darf nicht geworfen werden

Diese Beispielsätze stehen im *Present Tense*. In anderen Zeiten musst du die jeweiligen Ersatzformen von *can*, *must* und *may* verwenden. Du findest alles Wichtige zu diesen drei unvollständigen Hilfsverben im Abschnitt D dieses Buches.

Einige Formen, die du vielleicht häufiger benötigst, haben wir hier für dich zusammengestellt:

Helmets **must be worn** *.../*have to be worn* ...   *present tense*
    ... müssen getragen werden ...

Helmets **needn't be worn** *.../*don't have to be worn* ...
    ... müssen nicht getragen werden ...

    ... *had to be worn* ...   *past tense*
    ... mussten getragen werden ...

    ... *didn't have to be worn* ...
    ... mussten nicht getragen werden ...

Passiv

Fred can be found ... **present tense**
... kann gefunden werden ...

Fred can't be found ...
... kann nicht gefunden werden ...

Fred could be found ... **past tense**
... konnte gefunden werden ...

Fred couldn't be found ...
... konnte nicht gefunden werden ...

Die Ersatzformen klingen hier eher umständlich und werden daher kaum verwendet.

Mit der folgenden Übung kannst du überprüfen, ob du auch diesen Bereich des Passivs bereits beherrschst.

[1] to keep on the lead
[2] microwave (oven)
[3] to bandage (regular)
[4] paintings
[5] flash
[6] oysters
[7] to pull out a tooth

G10 *Übersetze ins Englische:*

1. Hunde müssen an der Leine[1] geführt werden.

   ....

2. Die Patienten dürfen von 16.00 bis 19.00 Uhr besucht werden.

   ....

3. Die Fenster konnten nicht geöffnet werden.

   ....

4. Rohe Eier dürfen nicht in der Mikrowelle[2] erhitzt werden.

   ....

5. Freds Bein musste verbunden[3] werden.

   ....

6. Die Gemälde[4] dürfen nicht mit Blitz[5] fotografiert werden.

   ....

7. Austern[6] können roh gegessen werden.

   ....

8. Gott sei Dank musste der Zahn nicht gezogen[7] werden!

   ....

4. Das persönliche Passiv

Zum Schluss hast du noch Gelegenheit, eine Form des Passivs zu üben, die sich vom Deutschen unterscheidet: das persönliche Passiv.
Aus dem folgenden Satz lässt sich – du weißt ja bereits wie – ganz leicht ein Passiv konstruieren:

A nice lady offered me a piece of cake.

Akkusativobjekt

A piece of cake was offered to me (by a nice lady).

Subjekt

Man nehme das Akkusativobjekt des Aktiv-Satzes und mache es zum Subjekt des Passiv-Satzes.

Es gibt aber noch eine weitere Möglichkeit:

A nice lady offered me a piece of cake.

Dativobjekt

I was offered a piece of cake (by a nice lady).

Subjekt

> Auch das **Dativobjekt** (wem oder was?) eines **Aktiv-Satzes** kann im **Passiv-Satz zum Subjekt** werden.

Im Deutschen kann man nicht sagen: Ich wurde ein Stück Kuchen angeboten. Vielmehr muss es heißen: Mir wurde ein Stück Kuchen angeboten.

Exercise G11 *Dazu gleich eine Übung:*

1. Granny told Tom an interesting story.

   Tom ....

2. Mr Brown had sold Mr Smith the old Ford.

   Mr Smith ....

3. A friendly gentleman showed me the way.

   I ....

4. One of her friends has sent Barbara a postcard from Australia.

   Barbara ....

5. The stewardess gave me a glass of orange juice.

   I ....

Passiv

Wie angekündigt, hier nun eine Übung zum Futur, in der auch gelegentlich ein persönliches Passiv vorkommt.

 A cycling tour through Ireland

The Greenfields from Boston are planning a two weeks' cycling tour through Ireland. Their bikes will be transported on the plane, together with the other baggage[1]. In Ireland someone will
- pick them up at Dublin airport,
- take them and the baggage to a guesthouse,
- give them special cycling maps,
- transport their baggage from one guesthouse to the next,
- book their rooms in advance,
- show them where to put their bikes,
- tell them where to find inns or coffee shops on the way.

[1] baggage – (Amer.) Gepäck

Cathy Greenfield is telling her friend Sue about the trip:

We will be picked up at Dublin airport.

We ....

We ....

Our baggage ....

Our rooms ....

We ....

We ....

Bevor du den gewohnten Abschlusstest absolvierst, solltest du noch einmal die verschiedenen Formen des Passivs wiederholen. Damit das Ganze nicht zu unübersichtlich wird, enthält die folgende Tabelle nur die *simple forms*; die *progressive forms* wurden hier nicht berücksichtigt.

Passiv

Exercise

 G13 *Ergänze die fehlenden Formen:*

past perfect	simple past	present perfect	simple present	future I
it had been stolen				
	he was found			
		we have been asked		
			she is seen	
				it will be sold
			it is made	
		it has been used		
	it was written			
they had been repaired				

Und wie am Ende jedes Kapitels kannst du auch jetzt wieder deine Kenntnisse überprüfen.

Test

1. Change the following sentences into the passive voice.
(Je 2 Punkte für jeden richtigen Satz, davon 1 Punkt für die richtige Verbform und 1 Punkt für den Rest)

a Dad will pick you up at the airport.

....

b Mr Brown has often repaired the car himself.

....

c People all over the world drink tea.

....

d Skyline Enterprises offered Mrs Barnes a leading position.

....

e David Bowie had written the soundtrack.

....

f The firemen had to rescue four people and a cat from the burning house.

....

2. Translate the following advert for the latest Hollywood film:
(Die maximale Punktzahl steht jeweils in Klammern.)

[1] creatures
[2] fast-food restaurant

Der spannendste Film, der jemals gemacht wurde!	(2)
Amerika wird von gefährlichen Wesen[1] angegriffen.	(2)
Sie wurden geschickt, um alle Schnellimbisse[2] mitzunehmen.	(2)
Wenn sie nicht aufgehalten werden können, wird New York zerstört werden!	(3)
Ein Held muss gefunden werden, der gegen diese Wesen kämpfen wird.	(2)
Er ist gefunden worden: Fred, der Terminator!	(1)

Testauswertung

My personal scoreboard:

24–19 "right" scores:
Brilliant! You did a really good job!
You know all the tenses well, and more than that – you use the passive as if it was the easiest thing in the world.

18–12 "right" scores:
That's a good score for such a difficult matter! If you had problems with the tenses, read chapter A. If you feel uneasy about the passive, do some of the exercises in this chapter again.

11–0 "right" scores:
Make sure you know how to form the tenses (Chapter A) before reading this chapter carefully again. Do all the exercises – then try the test again.

Word Power

Rechtschreibung
Spelling

Die englische Rechtschreibung ist nicht immer einfach. Hier findest du einige Tipps, wie du dir die richtige Schreibweise mancher Wörter besser einprägen kannst.

1. Lernposter
Es gibt einige Rechtschreibregeln bzw. Besonderheiten, die sich gut und übersichtlich auf einem selbst gefertigten Lernposter darstellen lassen.

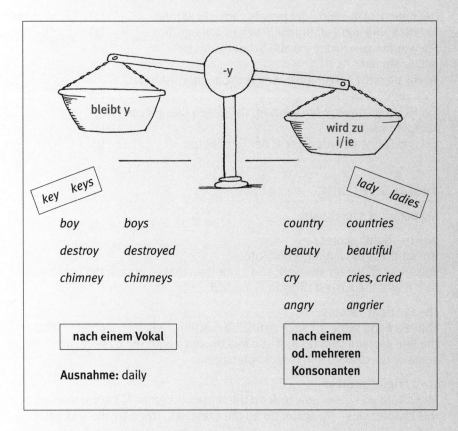

Wann immer dir ein Wort einfällt, das auf -y endet, kannst du dein Lernposter erweitern und z. B. kleine farbige Zettel darauf kleben (etwa gelbe für diejenigen Wörter, in denen das -y auch y bleibt, und grüne für Wörter, in denen das -y zu i/ie wird.

Probier's doch gleich mal aus! Vielleicht fallen dir zu jeder der beiden Gruppen je drei Wörter ein?!

2. Eselsbrücken

Damit du gleich von Anfang an die richtige Schreibung eines Wortes in deinem Gedächtnis speicherst, solltest du dir viele Eselsbrücken bauen. Je abenteuerlicher eine Merkhilfe, desto besser ist oft ihre Wirkung!

Hier einige Beispiele:

to spread
(sich) ausbreiten

Spread on the bread, Fred!

pole
Stab, Stange, Mast

edge
Rand, Kante

3. Lückentext oder -diktat

Fotokopiere (und vergrößere dabei) einen Text, in dem einige Wörter oder Ausdrücke vorkommen, deren Schreibung dir Schwierigkeiten bereitet. Schneide diese Wörter aus oder übermale sie mit einem schwarzen Stift.

Versuche, den Text später wieder zu vervollständigen, indem du die fehlenden Ausdrücke entweder gleich in die Lücken schreibst oder auf Zettel, die du auf die Lücken klebst.
Statt den Lückentext zu lesen, kannst du dir auch den vollständigen Text diktieren lassen. Dabei schreibst du die fehlenden Wörter in die Lücken.

Der Genitiv
The genitive

SECOND FLOOR
Men's Wear

FIRST FLOOR
Children's Wear
Teenagers' Corner

GROUND FLOOR
Ladies' Wear

Fred's new T-shirt

Der Genitiv oder „Besitzfall" wird gebraucht, wenn es um Besitz im weitesten Sinne geht. Oft haben wir es im Englischen mit einem *s*-Genitiv zu tun. Dabei wird an das betreffende Wort ein Apostroph und dann ein *s* angehängt. Manchmal steht der Apostroph aber auch nach dem *s*. Das klingt verwirrend, ist aber eigentlich ganz logisch. Es gibt nämlich eindeutige Regeln dafür – und genau diese Regeln wollen wir dir jetzt vorstellen.

1. Der *s*-Genitiv

's

Fred's new T-shirt *Mrs Bates's favourite hat* *the girl's shoes*
 or: *Mrs Bates' favourite hat*

Freds neues T-Shirt der Lieblingshut von die Schuhe des
 Frau Bates Mädchens

Regel

Bei **Personen im Singular** (auch bei Namen, die auf -s enden) fügst du im Genitiv ein **'s** an.

Genitiv

the dog's bone
der Knochen
des Hundes

the dog's bones
die Knochen
des Hundes

> Auch bei **Tieren im Singular** kannst du -'s anfügen. **Regel**

men's wear
Herrenbekleidung

children's shoes
Kinderschuhe

> Bei **unregelmäßigen Pluralformen** steht ebenfalls -'s. **Regel**

Australia's wildlife
Australiens wild
lebende Tiere

an hour's drive
eine einstündige
Fahrt

> Bei **Orts- und Ländernamen** kann -'s oder der *of*-Genitiv stehen. Verwende den *s*-Genitiv (-'s) auch bei **Zeitangaben im Singular**. **Regel**

Genitiv

Exercise

H1 Na, das kannst du gleich mal üben!

Übersetze:

1. Barbaras Bruder
2. das Nest des Vogels
3. der neue Präsident von Kanada
4. die Füße des Jungen
5. Männersocken
6. der Kopf des Schweins
7. eine einstündige Pause
8. Kinderspielsachen
9. die größte Stadt Deutschlands
10. der Hund unserer Nachbarin

Schauen wir uns nun die zweite Variante des *s*-Genitivs an: Es wird ein Apostroph an das bereits vorhandene *s* angehängt.

s'

girls' shoes
Mädchen-schuhe

the *Bakers'* dogs
die Hunde der Bakers

the *dogs'* bone
der Knochen der Hunde

the *dogs'* bones
die Knochen der Hunde

Regel

Bei **Personen und Tieren im Plural** wird bei **regelmäßiger Pluralform** (-s) ein **einfacher Apostroph** hinzugefügt.

Genitiv

*a **three hours'** drive*
eine dreistündige Fahrt

*in **two days'** time*
in zwei Tagen

> **Regel**
>
> Bei **Zeitangaben im Plural** steht ebenfalls -'s.

H2 *Auch hierzu eine kleine Übung:* **Exercise**

1. das neue Auto der Millers ....
2. die Ohren der Pferde ....
3. die Jacken der Zwillinge ....
4. eine zweistündige Verspätung[1] ....   [1] delay
5. Hundekekse ....
6. das Zimmer meiner Eltern ....
7. der Garten der Greens ....
8. eine vierstündige Fahrt ....
9. die Fahrräder meiner Schwestern ....
10. die Ohren der Kaninchen ....

Es gibt aber noch eine zweite Form des Genitivs – den sogenannten *of-*Genitiv. Wann sollst du diese Form verwenden?

2. Der *of*-Genitiv

of

the name of the game
der Name des Spiels

the colour of his hair
die Farbe seiner Haare

Regel: Bei **Dingen** verwendet man den *of*-Genitiv.

the shoes of the guy
who thinks he's John Wayne
die Schuhe des Typen,
der sich für John Wayne hält

the name of the lady
who lives next door
der Name der Dame,
die nebenan wohnt

Regel: Der *of*-Genitiv steht dann bei **Personen**, wenn eine **längere Erläuterung** folgt.

Exercise H3

1. der Name der Straße
2. die Dächer der Häuser
3. die Wurzeln der Bäume
4. das Auto der Leute, die letzte Woche hier eingezogen sind
5. die Farbe meines neuen Regenschirms
6. die Namen der Tiere, die in Australien leben

3. Der Genitiv ohne nachfolgendes Substantiv

Nicht immer steht der Genitiv mit einem nachfolgenden Substantiv (Hauptwort). Besonders in der gesprochenen Sprache wird es oft weggelassen.

Is this book Kevin's?
No, it's Jane's.
Gehört das Buch Kevin?
Nein, es gehört Jane.

This ball isn't mine.
Is it yours?
Dieser Ball gehört nicht mir.
Ist es deiner?

> **Regel**
> Das nachfolgende **Substantiv kann entfallen,** wenn klar ist, worauf sich der Genitiv bezieht.

Genitiv

*I went **to the doctor's** this morning.*
Ich bin heute morgen zum Arzt gegangen.

*I'm going to spend the weekend **at my aunt's**.*
Ich verbringe das Wochenende bei meiner Tante.

Regel

Auch bei **Geschäften**, **Ärzten** und **Privathäusern** fällt meist das entsprechende Substantiv *(shop, surgery, house, flat)* weg.

Alles klar? Die nächste Übung wartet auf dich.

Exercise

 Mrs Silverstone hat immer einen vollen Terminkalender. Übersetze, was sie so alles macht.

 Am Montagmorgen ging sie zum Bäcker und zum Metzger.

....

....

 Am Nachmittag war sie beim Zahnarzt und in der Apotheke.

....

....

 Sie verbrachte den Dienstagvormittag beim Friseur.

....

[1] Sportwagen = sports car

 Eine Dame fragte: „Ist der rote Sportwagen[1] Ihrer?"
Mrs Silverstone antwortete: „Nein, das ist nicht meiner, er gehört meinem Bruder."

....

....

 Von Mittwoch bis Samstag blieb sie bei ihrer Schwester.

....

4. Der „doppelte" Genitiv

Zum Schluss noch eine Besonderheit: Ein *of*-Genitiv und ein *s*-Genitiv bzw. ein Possessivpronomen (besitzanzeigendes Fürwort) können auch miteinander kombiniert werden.

a friend of mine
ein Freund von mir

a friend of my father's
ein Freund meines Vaters

> Der „doppelte" Genitiv macht hier deutlich, dass die jeweilige Person **mehrere** Freunde hat.
> Man könnte auch sagen: *one of my friends, one of my father's friends*

Regel

H5 Fred blättert in seinem Fotoalbum.
Vervollständige die Sätze:

Exercise

1. Das ist Julie, eine Freundin von mir aus Australien.

   That's Julie, ... from Australia.

2. Das ist Pete. Ein Nachbar von ihm gießt gerade die Blumen.

   That's Pete. .... is watering the flowers.

3. Charlies Onkel ist Feuerwehrmann. Das ist Charlie mit einigen Kollegen seines Onkels.

   Charlie's uncle is a fireman. That's Charlie with some colleagues

   ....

4. Und das ist Maggie. Jonglieren ist ein großes Hobby von ihr.

   And that's Maggie. Juggling is a great hobby ....

Genitiv

Bevor du dich an den Abschlusstest wagst, kannst du jetzt noch einmal überprüfen, ob alles „sitzt". In der folgenden Übung kommen alle Genitivformen vor.

H6 *Form sentences with the words – and use the correct form of the genitive.*
Be careful – the parts of the sentences are not in the right order!

1. the Millers/has got seats/new car/for seven people.

2. my room/are decorated/the walls/with lots of posters.

3. celebrated/a friend/his birthday/of mine/last Saturday.

4. brother/broke his leg/Linda/yesterday.

5. a/we have/break/twenty minutes/at 10.30.

6. the roof/has to be repaired/our neighbour/house.

7. the lady/is that/the purse/with the two poodles?

8. not/Jane/jacket/that's/it's/Diana.

9. clothes/are rather expensive/children/in this shop.

10. feathers/were glittering/the birds/in the sun.

11. had to go/to the dentist/my sister/this morning.

12. the Empire State Building/America/is/highest skyscrapers/one of.

Genitiv

Test

(Je 2 Punkte für jeden richtig übersetzten Ausdruck)

Complete the following sentences:

1. Birgit is going to Australia as an au-pair girl .... (in drei Wochen).

2. (Der Cousin ihres Vaters) .... lives in Melbourne with his wife and their two daughters.

3. Birgit will have to look after the kids and .... (die Hunde der Mädchen).

4. She has already seen .... (ein Foto des Hauses) with the two girls sitting on the doorstep.

5. (Der Name des Mädchens) .... with the long black hair is Mary-Ann,

6. and .... (der Name ihrer Schwester) is Catherine.

7. It's .... (ein zwanzigstündiger Flug) to Australia, and Birgit is a little afraid because she has never been so far away from home before.

8. (Eine Freundin von ihr) .... promised Birgit that she would write her a letter every week.

9. (Beim Arzt) .... Birgit read an interesting article in a magazine.

10. It was about .... (die Tierwelt Australiens). Birgit likes kangaroos, and she is looking forward to seeing lots of them in the Australian outback.

Genitiv

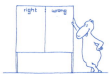

Testauswertung

My personal scoreboard:

20–15 "right" scores:
There is only one thing to say:

14–10 "right" scores:
You got most of the 's, s' and of-genitives right.
Some of the forms are a little tricky. Which were the ones you had problems with? Have another look at these parts of this chapter.

9–0 "right" scores:
What went wrong? Maybe you didn't read the German expressions carefully enough. Or you did the test without having done all the exercises in this chapter?!

mentor Lernhilfe

Englisch
7./8. Klasse

Grammatik und Wortschatz: Teil 1

Astrid Stannat
Dieter D'Zenit
Willi Mey †

Lösungsteil

In Zusammenarbeit mit Langenscheidt

mentor
Eine Klasse besser.

Lösungen

Kapitel A

A1 — Seite 9

simple past	future I	simple present
regelmäßige Verben: -ed an die Grundform unregelmäßige Verben: 2. Form	will + Grundform des Verbs im Mündlichen: 'll + Grundform	Grundform des Verbs 3. Pers. Singular *(he, she, it)*: -s wird angehängt

past perfect
had + 3. Form
(-ed oder
(unregelm. Form)

present perfect
I, you, we, they have + 3. Form
he, she, it has + 3. Form

A2 — Seite 10

gehen: go – went – gone
liegen: lie – lay – lain
vergessen: forget – forgot – forgotten
schreiben: write – wrote – written
ziehen: draw – drew – drawn
werfen: throw – threw – thrown
wissen: know – knew – known
singen: sing – sang – sung
trinken: drink – drank – drunk
geben: give – gave – given
essen: eat – ate – eaten
fallen: fall – fell – fallen

A3 — Seite 11

past perfect	simple past	present perfect	simple present	future
he had played	he played	he has played	he plays	he will play
she had gone	she went	she has gone	she goes	she will go
I had opened	I opened	I have opened	I open	I will open
we had come	we came	we have come	we come	we will come
I had tried	I tried	I have tried	I try	I will try
he had written	he wrote	he has written	he writes	he will write
she had seen	she saw	she has seen	she sees	she will see
they had spent	they spent	they have spent	they spend	they will spend
she had read	she read	she has read	she reads	she will read
it had rained	it rained	it has rained	it rains	it will rain

A4 — Seite 12

After I had woken up, I got up.
After I had got up, I washed.
After I had washed, I put on my clothes.
After I had put on my clothes, I went downstairs into the kitchen.
After I had gone downstairs into the kitchen, I had breakfast.
After I had had breakfast, I went into the garden.
After I had gone into the garden, I played football.
After I had played football, I read a book.
After I had read a book, I wrote a letter.
After I had written a letter, I bought a pound of apples.

Lösungen Kapitel A

Fortsetzung

After I had bought a pound of apples, I fed the horses.
After I had fed the horses, I drew a picture.
After I had drawn a picture, I sang a song.
After I had sung a song, I repaired the car.
After I had repaired the car, I watched TV.
After I had watched TV, I went to bed.

past perfect	simple past	present perfect	simple present	future
we hadn't known	we didn't know	we haven't known	we don't know	we won't know
it hadn't helped	it didn't help	it hasn't helped	it doesn't help	it won't help
she hadn't given	she didn't give	she hasn't given	she doesn't give	she won't give
you hadn't won	you didn't win	you haven't won	you don't win	you won't win
I hadn't moved	I didn't move	I haven't moved	I don't move	I won't move
he hadn't forgotten	he didn't forget	he hasn't forgotten	he doesn't forget	he won't forget
they hadn't bought	they didn't buy	they haven't bought	they don't buy	they won't buy
we hadn't seen	we didn't see	we haven't seen	we don't see	we won't see
she hadn't spent	she didn't spend	she hasn't spent	she doesn't spend	she won't spend
I hadn't slept	I didn't sleep	I haven't slept	I don't sleep	I won't sleep

past perfect	simple past	present perfect	simple present	future
had he liked?	did he like?	has he liked?	does he like?	will he like?
had you caught?	did you catch?	have you caught?	do you catch?	will you catch?
had he forgotten?	did he forget?	has he forgotten?	does he forget?	will he forget?
had they gone?	did they go?	have they gone?	do they go?	will they go?
had we hit?	did we hit?	have we hit?	do we hit?	will we hit?
had they seen?	did they see?	have they seen?	do they see?	will they see?
had you told?	did you tell?	have you told?	do you tell?	will you tell?
had I opened?	did I open?	have I opened?	do I open?	will I open?
had he taken?	did he take?	has he taken?	does he take?	will he take?
had she lost?	did she lose?	has she lost?	does she lose?	will she lose?

Hier einige weitere Vorschläge:

I didn't move: The bear was only about twenty metres away from me. I didn't move. ...

it will rain: Our neighbour is washing his car. I'm pretty sure it will rain in the afternoon. It always rains after he has washed his car.

do you catch? You always go fishing at the weekends. Do you ever catch any fish – or do you just go fishing for the fun of it?

1. A bad day for Mike

Yesterday <u>wasn't</u> Mike's lucky day. He <u>had forgotten</u> to set his alarm clock the night before, so he <u>slept</u> too long. As he <u>didn't have</u> time for breakfast he just <u>made</u> himself a sandwich that he <u>wanted</u> to eat on his way to school. But then his dog <u>ate</u> the sandwich because Mike <u>had put</u> it on the kitchen table!
At school he <u>wrote</u> a German test – and of course he <u>hadn't revised</u> the new words. But on top of all that he <u>found</u> out that he <u>had</u> toothpaste on his shirt after he <u>had talked</u> to Michelle, the pretty girl who seemed to fancy him.

2.

We will arrive at the airport in time.
Judy gets up at five o'clock every day.
The Greens haven't sold their car.
Brian doesn't have pancakes for breakfast every day.
Had they met before?
Janet bought that dress in New York.

Pictures and Words

Folgende Autoteile solltest du kennzeichnen:

windscreen – *Windschutzscheibe*
mudguard – *Kotflügel*
steering wheel – *Lenkrad*
bumper – *Stoßstange*
boot – *Kofferraum*
rear lights – *Rücklichter*

front lights – *vordere Scheinwerfer*
petrol tank – *Tank*
number plate – *Nummernschild*
bonnet – *Motorhaube*
tyre – *Reifen*
windscreen wipers – *Scheibenwischer*

Kapitel B

What's your name?
What are your hobbies?
Are you good at school?

My name is Fred.
I like reading, swimming, and waterskiing.
Well, I'm quite good at languages, but maths isn't my cup of tea!

I'm from Adelaide. That's

Where are you from?
in the south of Australia.

The "Spice Girls" are my favourite group but I also like Australian bands like "Men at Work".
I'm fourteen.
You mean that traditional Aborigine instrument?
No, I'm afraid I can't.

What kind of music do you like?

How old are you?
Can you play the didgeridoo?

Lösungen Kapitel B

Seite 21 B2

Wenn du wissen möchtest,
ob das Mädchen oder der Junge   dann müsstest du fragen:

1. eine(n) Brieffreund(in) hat,   Have you got a pen-friend?
2. gerne Reisen unternimmt,   Do you like travelling?
3. schon mal in Deutschland war,   Have you ever been to Germany?
5. eine gute Sportlerin/ein guter   Are you good at sports?
   Sportler ist,
5. ein Haustier hat,   Have you got a pet?
6. in einer großen Stadt wohnt,   Do you live in a big city?
7. gerne Techno-Musik hört,   Do you like listening to Techno music?
8. Geschwister hat,   Have you got any brothers or sisters?
9. am Nachmittag Schule hat,   Have you got school in the afternoon?
10. schon mal die Schule geschwänzt   Have you ever played truant?
    hat,
11. mit dir zum Strand gehen will,   Would you like to go to the beach
                                            with me?
12. mit dir in Verbindung bleiben   Would you like to keep in touch with
    möchte.   me?

Seite 24 B3

Die folgenden Sätze stellen jeweils nur eine von mehreren Möglichkeiten dar.
Vielleicht hast du eine andere Formulierung gewählt:

1. Would you like to come to my birthday party?
2. Do you think you could lend me your air matress?
3. How about spending our next holiday in Ireland?
4. Could you pass me the salt, please?
5. Let's go to the hotel disco tonight!
6. We'd be very pleased if you and your parents came to dinner next Friday.

Seite 25 B4

Hello, Mrs Winkler! This is
Fred speaking. Can I talk to Jörg?

    Hello, Fred. I'll go and get him. Hold on!

Thank you.

    Hello, Fred. It's Jörg here.

Hello, Jörg. How are you?

    I'm fine, thanks. And you?

I'm alright. Listen, Jörg. We are
planning to have a barbecue next
Saturday. I'd like you to come, too.
Are you free on Saturday evening?

    Oh Fred, could you speak a little more
    slowly, please? Well, I have a football
    match on Saturday.

Oh, what a pity!
At what time is the match?

    At five o'clock.

You could come after the match,
couldn't you?

    Yes, if that's o. k. with you.

That's great! I hope your team will win.
I'll keep my fingers crossed for you!

    Thank you, Fred! I'm sure that'll help!
    Thanks for ringing and see you on Saturday, then!

See you on Saturday. Bye!

Lösungen Kapitel B

Hier ist ... /Hier spricht ...	a) This is ... speaking.
	b) It's ... here.
Kann ich ... sprechen?	Can I talk to ...?
Bleib dran!	Hold on!
Könntest du bitte etwas langsamer sprechen?	Could you speak a little more slowly, please?
Wie geht's dir?	How are you?
Mir geht's gut.	a) I'm fine, thanks.
	b) I'm alright.
Hast du am Samstag Zeit?	Are you free on Saturday?
Danke, dass du angerufen hast.	Thanks for ringing.
Bis Samstag!	See you on Saturday!

B5 *Seite 27*

Do you understand me?	Yes, I do.
May/Can I ask you some questions?	Yes, you may/can.
Are you from Mars?	No, I'm not.
Did you come by spacecraft?	No, I didn't.
Do your parents know where you are?	Yes, they do.
Have you got any friends here?	Yes, I have.
Would you like something to eat?	No, thank you.
Could you please tell me something about your planet?	Yes, of course.
Will you go back to your planet soon?	No, I won't.

B6 *Seite 28*

1. Does Jack live in London?
2. Did I lock the door last night?
3. Does your brother speak Italian?
4. Did you go out last Saturday?
5. Did the Millers spend their holidays in Florida last year?
6. Do you always get up so early?
7. Do your parents like dogs?
8. Did Jenny do well in her last English test?

B7 *Seite 30*

Who is that man? – Charles Breakneck!
When did you last see him? – Last Friday.
Where was that? – In the Penguin Bar.
What was he wearing? – A coat, I think.
What coat? – A leather coat.
What colour? – Black.
How long did he stay there? – The whole evening, until one o'clock, I think.
How much money did he spend there? – I don't know, but I'm sure it was more than £ 100.
How many people were there that night? – Oh, it was quite crowded, more than 50, I think.
How often do you normally go there? – Twice a week.
Why do you go there? – I like the atmosphere. And I like to meet people.
Who do you meet there? – Friends.

Lösungen Kapitel B

Seite 31

1. a) Who saw the two robbers at Victoria Station?
   b) Who did a fifteen-year-old boy see?

2. a) What hit my teacher on the head?
   b) Who did the apple hit on the head?

3. a) Who likes Mrs Brown?
   b) Who do all the pupils like?

4. a) Who often sees flying saucers in her garden?
   b) What does Helen often see in her garden?

5. a) Who loves Matthew?
   b) Who does Judith love?

Seite 32

Where do you live?
Where were you yesterday evening?
Who saw you there?
How long did you stay there?
Where is your car key?
Do you know the woman on the photo?
Where does she live?
When did you last see her?

Seite 32 **B10**

If you ask me – people watch too much television!
– I agree with you.

In my opinion all those sitcoms on TV are complete rubbish!
– Oh no, that's not true! I really enjoy watching "Roseanne".

When the weather is nice, I don't like sitting in front of the goggle-box.
– Neither do I!

I think there shouldn't be any commercials on TV.
– Well, of course, but on the other hand, you wouldn't want to have pay TV only, or would you?

Seite 34

Hier einige Vorschläge:

It's good to learn a foreign language.
– I think so, too. When you go on holiday, you can talk to the people whose language you are learning.
Homework is necessary.
– O.K., only practice makes perfect. But on the other hand there is too much homework sometimes.
Girls shouldn't play football.
– That's rubbish! I don't agree at all! If a girl likes playing football, why on earth shouldn't she?

Seite 35

1. In my opinion three months of school holidays are too long!
2. I don't think so!/I don't agree with you! Children and teenagers need this time to relax.
3. As far as I know, most pupils sleep during the lessons. I think that's enough!
4. I just can't agree with you!/I don't think so! A school day is really exhausting, and afterwards the pupils/students have to do their homework.

5. Rubbish! There's no school at the weekends, and there are holidays every few weeks. The kids just don't know what to do with their spare/free time.
6. That's not true. We simply need time for our family, our friends and our hobbies. I'm sure that you don't want to work every day, either!

Test   Seite 36

(1.)
1. Are you American?
2. When do you get up in the morning?
3. Where do you live?
4. Could you please lend me your bike?
5. What did you do last Saturday?
6. Who wrote "Frankenstein"?
7. Have you ever been to Malta?
8. Where does your brother work?

(2.)
1. As far as I know, most school uniforms are dark blue, grey or dark green.
2. In my opinion/I think everybody should be able to decide for himself/herself what he/she wants to wear.
3. That's just what I think. If you ask me – school uniforms look boring.
4. Yes, but on the other hand the school is no disco! A lot of boys and girls spend hours in front of their wardrobe!
5. I agree with you completely! For many kids clothes are extremely important – too important!

Word power   Seite 37

Arbeit mit dem Wörterbuch I
1. Gangart: walk
2. Weg: way
3. Flur: corridor
4. im Flugzeug: aisle
5. beim Essen: course
6. beim Auto: gear
7. Verlauf: course

Postkarte: postcard
Landkarte: map
Fahrkarte: ticket
Speisekarte: menu

Eisenbahn: train
Schachzug: move

Kochrezept: recipe
Rezept v. Arzt: prescription

Geldinstitut: bank
Sitzbank: bench, seat

Bild (allg.):   picture
Gemälde: painting
Foto: photo(graph)
Zeichnung: drawing

Kapitel C

Seite 40

Past Perfect (Simple):	he had caught a dead whale
Past Perfect (Progressive):	which had been drifting
Past (Simple):	When he wanted to reel in …
	he got the shock of his life
	It took me about …
Past (Progressive):	Mr J. Gallagher … was fishing …
Present Perfect (Simple):	this is the biggest "fish" I've ever caught
Present Perfect (Progressive):	I've been going fishing for more than 15 years

Seite 42

– Where did you spend your holidays?
– We were in Spain.
– Was it nice?
– Yes, it was. We had a nice holiday home near the beach. In the morning we often visited some sights and in the afternoon we went to the beach and played volleyball or swam in the sea.
– Did you meet any nice people?
– Yes, there was a family from Hamburg with two girls. One was 14, the other one was 12. We did a lot of things together.
– What was the food like?
– Most of the time we cooked our own meals. Every few days we went to a restaurant and ate some typical Spanish food. Only once I had something I didn't like. Apart from that it was always very tasty.
– By the way – many thanks for your postcard! I got it yesterday.
– Only yesterday? I wrote it more than two weeks ago!

Seite 44

Oh, yes, we have often gone (been) there.
And we have already spent some weeks in New York.
Yes, we have also sailed across the Atlantic Ocean.
And we have flown to Japan.
Have you ever crossed the Sahara desert on the back of a camel?
No, we have never done that before. But we don't like the idea.
Have you ever climbed Mount Everest?
No, we haven't climbed it yet. But I think it's too dangerous.
We have already watched kiwis in New Zealand!
No, we have never stayed at home. (No, we have never done that.)

Seite 47

Have you ever eaten bacon and eggs?
Yes, I ate it on the boat last week.

Have you ever drunk English tea?
No, I haven't drunk it yet. Yesterday in London I had coffee.

Have you ever tasted grilled sausages?
I have often had them at home. But I have never tried them for breakfast.

Have you ever eaten sugar puffs?
Sugar puffs? No! I have never eaten them. But I would like to try them.

Lösungen Kapitel C

C5 *Seite 48*

1. Cathy to her sister Sabrina: I was having a shower when someone switched off the light!
Sabrina: Oops – I'm sorry. I didn't know you <u>were having</u> a shower. I thought it was Dad!
2. Frank <u>was having</u> a shower when someone opened the door, ran towards him and jumped at him. – It was his dog Prince!
3. Tom: While we <u>were having</u> a shower after the match, our coach was still outside on the field. He couldn't believe that we had actually won.
4. While the girls <u>were having</u> a shower, some boys tried to peep through the key-hole. But the sports teacher caught them and they got into real trouble!

C6 *Seite 49*

1. Tom and Judy were playing tennis.
2. The Johnsons were having a barbecue.
3. Fred was riding on his bike. (Fred was cycling.)
4. Mr Greenfield was washing his car.
5. Linda, Joan and Kevin were watching a film at the cinema.
6. Our neighbour's cat was sleeping on a (garden) chair.

C7 *Seite 49*

1. The pupils <u>were throwing</u> scraps of paper at each other when the teacher <u>came</u> in.
2. While the Barristers <u>were having</u> dinner, there <u>was</u> a knock at the door.
3. Sally <u>was eating</u> a banana when a monkey suddenly <u>jumped</u> on her shoulder.
4. The lights <u>went</u> out while we <u>were playing</u> cards.
5. While Sherlock Holmes, the famous detective, <u>was looking</u> at some pictures, he <u>had</u> an idea.
6. Fred <u>was reading</u> a ghost story when he suddenly <u>heard</u> footsteps.

C8 *Seite 52*

For three days.
For two hours.
Since last Tuesday.
Since yesterday.
For two weeks.

C9 *Seite 52*

Hier einige Möglichkeiten:

For two weeks.
Since my last birthday.
For three years.
For six months.
Since last Christmas.
…

C10 *Seite 53*

I have been waiting for him …
you have been waiting
he/she has been waiting
we have been waiting
you have been waiting
they have been waiting

Lösungen Kapitel C + D

Seite 54
1. Mr Brown has been working in the garden since this morning.
2. Carol has been washing her car since five o'clock.
3. Ann has been watching TV for half an hour.
4. Tom's grandpa has been reading the newspaper since breakfast.
5. Susan has been writing a letter since she came home from school.
6. Mr Standish has been preparing the dinner for two hours.
7. Fred has been suffering from stomach-ache since he ate that lovely cake.
8. Tom and Peter have been playing chess for three hours.

Seite 55   Test
1. We've been waiting here for two hours!
2. I've never been to the Tower of London (before) – and now it's closed!
3. Did you buy this hat at Portobello Market yesterday?
4. We were (just) going to the bus stop when it started to rain.
5. I have had this umbrella since I was in London in April.
6. He has been standing here since six o'clock!

Word power
Seite 57

Hören und Sprechen

d oder t?	bed	*Bett*	bet	*Wette, wetten*
	tie	*binden, Krawatte*	die	*sterben*
	tent	*Zelt*	tend	*neigen*

b oder p?	bath	*Bad*	path	*Pfad, Weg*
	pack	*packen*	back	*Rücken, zurück*
	pig	*Schwein*	big	*groß*

g oder c?	guard	*Wächter*	card	*Karte*
	coat	*Mantel*	goat	*Ziege*
	came	*kam*	game	*Spiel*

Kapitel D

Seite 59
He is able to walk without any help.
He is able to switch on the radio.
He is able to drink from a cup.
He is able to build a tower with his bricks.

Seite 60
He couldn't walk without any help.
He couldn't switch on the radio.
He couldn't drink from a cup.
He couldn't build a tower with his bricks.
He wasn't able to walk without any help.
He wasn't able to switch on the radio.
He wasn't able to drink from a cup.
He wasn't able to build a tower with his bricks.

Lösungen Kapitel D

D3 Seite 61

1. My penfriend Fiona { can / is able to } speak a little German.
2. I { can't / 'm not allowed to } go to the concert with you …
3. The hippo { could / was able to } juggle with four balls.
4. … – he { can / is allowed to } go camping with us.
5. On the motorways you { couldn't / weren't allowed to } drive more than 70 mph.

D4 Seite 62

1. You { may / are allowed to } use this door only in case of emergency.
2. You { may not / are not allowed to } enter the road.
3. You { may not / are not allowed to } overtake cars, but
   you { may / are allowed to } overtake tractors.
4. You { may / are allowed to } bring your dog to the zoo, but you must keep it on the lead.
5. You { may not / are not allowed to } smoke here.

D5 Seite 63

We were allowed to listen to music in our rooms …
We weren't allowed to make any noise after ten.
There was a little lake nearby, but I wasn't allowed to go swimming there!
We were allowed to go to the public swimming-bath …
They had quite a number of bicycles and go-carts, and we were allowed to use them …
On the last day my friend Chris wanted to go shopping to the town centre. He wasn't allowed to go alone, so I went with him.

D6 Seite 64

First I have to do the shopping for her.
Then I have to fetch her some medicine from the chemist's.
After that I have to make her some tea.
And then I have to feed Tiffy, her cat.
When I come home I have to do my homework.

D7 Seite 64

She has to do the shopping for her.
Then she has to fetch her some medicine from the chemist's.
After that she has to make her some tea.
And then she has to feed Tiffy, her grandma's cat.
When she comes home, she has to do her homework.

Lösungen Kapitel D

Seite 64 · D8

First we had to do the shopping.
Then we had to fetch some medicine from the chemist's.
After that we had to make Grandma some tea.
And then we had to feed Tiffy.
When I came home, I had to do my homework.

Seite 66 · D9

I don't have to hurry to catch the bus.
I don't have to do any homework in the afternoon.
I don't have to write any tests.
I don't have to wear my school uniform.
I don't have to go to bed at eight.

I needn't hurry to catch the bus.
I needn't do any homework in the afternoon.
I needn't write any tests.
I needn't wear my school uniform.
I needn't go to bed at eight.

He doesn't have to hurry to catch the bus.
He doesn't have to do any homework in the afternoon.
He doesn't have to write any tests.
He doesn't have to wear his school uniform.
He doesn't have to go to bed at eight.

Seite 67 · D10

You mustn't smoke too much.
I needn't/don't have to get up early tomorrow. There is no school.
You needn't/don't have to write Tom a letter, he will be here tomorrow.
But Margret, you mustn't hit your little brother!
Bob, you mustn't forget to answer Henry's letter.
Henry, you mustn't drink so much Coke.
You needn't/don't have to eat all that pudding if you are not hungry.
You mustn't forget to write to me soon.
You needn't/don't have to feed the dog. I've already done it.

Seite 68 · D11

Hier einige Möglichkeiten:

Last week Angie had to water the flowers. She also had to clear the table.
She didn't have to lay the table. And she didn't have to feed the rabbits, either.
On Sunday she had to go for a walk with Scruffy.

Chris had to go for a walk with Scruffy on Tuesday, Wednesday and Friday,
he didn't have to go on the other days.
Dad and Chris had to lay the table. They didn't have to clear the table.

Seite 69 · D12

There is a small zoo in our town. Last week I <u>was allowed to</u> go there with my sister.
My father <u>couldn't/wasn't able to</u> come with us, he <u>had to</u> work, so we <u>had to</u> take
the bus. I <u>was allowed to</u> take my brother's camera with me but <u>I had to</u> promise him
to be very careful.
When we reached the entrance we first <u>had to</u> buy the tickets. My sister <u>was allowed
to</u> visit the zoo for half the price, as she is only eight years old. First we went to the
monkeys. There was a sign: You <u>mustn't</u> feed the animals. The keeper told us that
people who fed the monkeys <u>had to</u> pay a high fine.
My sister likes the hippopotamus very much. She was very happy when she <u>was</u>

<u>allowed to</u> help the keeper to feed it. I had to take a picture of her in front of the pool. We <u>were allowed to</u> ride on the elephant that carries visitors through the zoo. At six o'clock we <u>had to</u> leave the zoo.

D13 Seite 70

they will be able to understand

we will have to speak
we won't have to speak

I will be allowed to send
I won't be allowed to send

D14 Seite 71

1. Will we be able to see Xenos from there?
2. No, you won't be able to see Xenos … But there will be a video call every ten days, and you will be able to see and talk to your family then.
3. Do you think we will have to stay inside the buildings all the time?
4. When it rains or snows, we will have to wear special clothes.
5. Will we have to go to school every day?
6. No. We will not have to go to school at the weekends …
7. Is it true that we will not be allowed to speak Xenophonic at school?
8. That's right. We will have to speak Earthian at school. But we will be allowed to meet once a week and speak our own language then.
9. I hope I will be able to play it …
10. I'm sure you will be allowed to join the school baseball team.

Test   Seite 72

1. … I wasn't allowed to go to school for a/one week.
2. Next year my brother will be able to swim.
3. You needn't/don't have to wait for me.
4. I couldn't/wasn't able to ride a bike at the age of six (when I was six).
5. Mr Brown will have to wait for two hours.
6. In a lot of/many offices the employees are not allowed to/may not smoke.
7. Jack must/has to look after his little brother today.
8. Susan will not/won't be able to play volleyball tomorrow.

Word power
Seite 74

Nie wieder sprachlos!

Die folgenden Erklärungen sind Vorschläge:

1. Students/Pupils can get cheaper tickets if they show their student's card (ID card).
2. You mustn't go into the shop with rollerblades.
3. Children under eight can only go in with their mother or father.
4. Don't park here. If you do, you have to pay 80 Deutschmarks.
5. You put it on when you want to look at things under water. (snorkel)
6. It's a small piece of metal. You can fasten papers together with it. (paper clip)
7. You can dig holes into the ground with it. (spade)
8. It's an animal that lives in the sea. It is shaped like a star. (starfish)
9. Before it becomes a frog, it's a small creature with a black head and a long tail. (tadpole)
10. You can put something in it. It has got a wheel and two handles to lift and push it with. (wheelbarrow)
11. You need it if you want to receive lots of channels with your TV set. (satellite dish)
12. Athletes can jump very high with a long stick. (pole vaulting)

Kapitel E

Seite 77 E1

	direct speech wörtliche Rede	reported speech indirekte Rede
englischer Satz	Granny said: "I've lost my hearing aid."	Granny said she had lost her hearing aid.
deutscher Satz	Oma sagte: „Ich habe mein Hörgerät verloren."	Oma sagte, sie habe ihr Hörgerät verloren.

Seite 78 E2

	direct speech	reported speech
Verb Tense	needs simple present	needed simple past
Verb Tense	keeps simple present	kept simple past
Verb Tense	were wasted simple past	had been wasted past perfect
Verb Tense	have criticised present perfect	had criticised past perfect

Seite 80 E3

John's mother rang me up an hour ago. She said he was very sorry that he couldn't come to the party. She told me (that) he had been taken to hospital. There had been a football match at the school this morning. It had been the final of the school championship. She said (that) John had been running to get the ball when he had slipped, fallen and broken his ankle. Fortunately, his leg didn't hurt too badly. She also said he would stay in hospital for two days and he wouldn't be able to go to school for at least a week.

Seite 81 E4

1. He said (that) he had had a fight with a kangaroo.
2. David told Steve (that) the birds were flying north.
3. The man behind the desk said to David (that) he had tried to phone him at least ten times.
4. Helen said (that) she was sure that the two men would be found.
5. Jim said to the fireman (that) he needed a helmet and an axe.
6. He added (that) something had to be done.
7. The reporter said (that) nobody had been killed in the fire.

Lösungen Kapitel E

E5 — Seite 83

1. Last week I visited Tony and his family. Tony said (that) there were no kids in their neighbourhood there.
2. He explained to me that his new school was more than five miles away.
3. And he said that his new classmates were really nice. Some of them had asked him to join the football team.
4. Then he told me (that) he was going to a school party the next day.
5. He also told me (that) he had been at the sports centre the previous day. He said it was great. He had never seen anything like that before.

E6 — Seite 86

The first thing we wanted to know was how many hours per day the pupils spent in front of the "box".
We asked them what they had watched the day before/the previous day and if/whether there were any programmes they watched regularly.
We also wanted to find out if/whether they never/sometimes/often switched channels in the middle of a programme.
Of course we asked how many TV sets there were in their house/flat and if/whether they had got a TV set of their own.
Apart from that we wanted to know if/whether they had ever switched off the telly because they hadn't liked the programme and what they did during commercial breaks.

E7 — Seite 87

1. The procurer wanted to know whether I could sing.
2. He asked me in which plays I had already acted.
3. Then he wanted to know if I was interested in a role in advertising.
4. At the end of the interview he asked me whether I liked cats.

E8 — Seite 90

1. First, Tim wanted me to help him with his maths homework.
2. Then Grandma asked me to take a letter to the letterbox.
3. The worst thing was that Mum ordered me to tidy up my room.
4. Then Andy came in and asked me to draw an elephant for him.
5. When I said goodbye, Dad told me not to come home too late!

E9 — Seite 90

Well, first Tim wanted Ann to help him with his maths homework.
Then her grandmother asked her to take a letter to the letterbox.
The worst thing was that her mum ordered her to tidy up her room.
Then Andy came in and asked her to draw an elephant for him.
When she said goodbye, her dad told her not to come home too late!

Test — Seite 91

1.
"Yes, he called me the day before yesterday. He said he was ringing from Paris and it was a beautiful city. He told me that he had already seen the Eiffel Tower. The previous day/The day before they had gone to Versailles, that famous castle where the French kings had lived. Rupert said that there was gold everywhere, but he hadn't seen any bathrooms! He then explained to me that he would be in Rome the following/next day. A bus would take them to the most interesting sights. The last thing he said was that he had already taken hundreds of photos and that he had to go because they were meeting at the Louvre at two o'clock."

Lösungen Kapitel E + F

Seite 92 **Test**

2.
a Shirley asked her friend if/whether he/she liked her dress.
b The teacher said to Mary/told Mary to repeat the sentence.
c The gangster ordered the old lady to give him her handbag.
d The policeman asked the visitor where he had seen the man.
e Lisa's new classmates wanted to know if/whether she had already been to the school cafeteria.
f Mrs Scott told her little son not to throw the peas on the floor.

Word power
Seite 94

Arbeit mit dem Wörterbuch II

The gangsters were put behind bars.	*hinter Gitter*
He was engaged as a foreman.	*eingestellt*
He's not married but engaged.	*verlobt*
The line is engaged.	*Die Leitung ist besetzt.*
She was moved to tears.	*zu Tränen gerührt*
They moved to Munich.	*umziehen*
Don't move!	*sich bewegen*
What's the name of that famous pop star?	*Berühmtheit*
Starring Jodie Foster.	*in der Hauptrolle*
What do the stars say for today?	*Sterne, Horoskop*
We could see the moon and the stars.	*Sterne*
Your hands are dirty.	*Hände*
The child is in good hands.	*in guten Händen*
He worked as a farm-hand.	*Arbeiter*
The hour hand pointed to twelve.	*Zeiger*

Kapitel F

Seite 97

There is somebody/someone/something in the car.
Give me some apples, please.
The camera must be somewhere.
I want something to drink.
There are some sausages left.
Somebody/Someone/Something is behind you.
Let's meet somewhere else.
I've just bought some cheese.
Something is wrong with my watch.

I don't know anybody/anyone here.
Is there any money left?
Has anybody/anyone got a hanky?
Have you seen him anywhere?
Is anything wrong?
I haven't got any sugar.
That doesn't make any sense.
Anything else?
I haven't got any friends.

Seite 98

1. The box is empty. There isn't anything in it.
2. There are some pencils on the writing-desk.
3. I need somebody/someone to help me with the washing-up.
4. You can phone me at any time.
5. Why don't we go somewhere else?
6. Can you see my purse anywhere?
7. Would you like some sandwiches?

 Seite 99

1. There isn't anything in it.
2. We can't see it anywhere.
3. There aren't any stamps on the letter.
4. There wasn't anybody/anyone in the room.
5. He doesn't do anything all day.

F4 **Seite 100**

1. Every
2. Each
3. each
4. every

baseball

F5 **Seite 101**

1. many/a lot of
2. many/a lot of
3. a lot of
4. a lot of/lots of
5. much
6. a lot of/lots of

F6 **Seite 102**

1. little
2. few/a few
3. a little
4. a little
5. a few
6. a little

Test **Seite 102**

1. Have you got much/a lot of work to do this afternoon?
2. I'm sorry, I haven't got any coke. But there is some milk in the fridge.
3. Gloria and Juliet go jogging together every Saturday.
4. Would you like some more tea?
5. You can take any bus from this stop.
6. Ms Redgrave has five cats. Each of her cats has a basket of its own.
7. We didn't have much time, so we only wrote a few/some postcards.
8. I was a little surprised …

Lösungen Kapitel F + G

Word power
Seite 104

Lesen

collector	Sammler	investigate	untersuchen, Ermittlungen anstellen
forgery	Fälschung	chemical	chemisch

collector	collect	fame	famous
painting	paint	follower	follow
knowledge	know	changeable	change
meaningful	meaning	talkative	talk

chemical	chemisch	shoulder blade	Schulterblatt
information	Information	politician	Politiker
decoration	Dekoration	repair	reparieren
organize	organisieren	mass media	Massenmedien

Kapitel G

Seite 106

1. When Fred came to the site this morning three walls had already been finished. (true)
2. The cement was brought by a big cement mixer truck. (false)
3. Most of the windows have already been put in. (false)
4. Tomorrow the house will be finished. (false)
5. Heavy parts are lifted by a crane. (true)

Seite 106

1. ...three walls had already been built.   past perfect
2. The cement was brought ...   simple past/past tense
3. ...the windows have already been put in.   present perfect
4. ...the house will be finished.   future I
5. Heavy parts are lifted ...   simple present/present tense

Seite 107

1. Engines are repaired.
2. Tyres are pumped up.
3. Brakes are checked.
4. Plugs are changed.
5. Tanks are filled./The tank is filled.
6. Cars are washed.
7. Windscreen wipers are repaired.
8. The oil is checked.

Seite 109

1. The tyres are being changed.
2. The car is being washed.
3. The radio is being repaired.
4. The oil is being checked.
5. The lights are being tested.

Seite 109

1. 52 persons were injured.
2. A bus was swept off the road.
3. Cars were overturned.
4. Trees were uprooted.
5. A bridge was destroyed.
6. The fire department was called twenty-seven times last night.

Lösungen Kapitel G

 Seite 110

1. The living room window has been broken.
2. The wardrobe has been opened.
3. All the clothes have been thrown on the floor.
4. Papers have been torn to pieces.
5. The TV set has been smashed up.
6. The silver candle sticks have been taken away.
7. The stamp collection has been stolen.
8. A bottle of whisky has been drunk.
9. The radio has been damaged.

 Seite 110

1. The window had been broken.
2. The wardrobe had been opened.
3. All the clothes had been thrown on the floor.
4. Papers had been torn to pieces.
5. The TV set had been smashed up.
6. The silver candle sticks had been taken away.
7. The stamp collection had been stolen.
8. A bottle of whisky had been drunk.
9. The radio had been damaged.

 Seite 112

Tom is writing a letter.	active	present
This machine was built in the USA.	passive	past
This parcel has been opened before.	passive	present perfect
My friend has often been in London.	active	present perfect
These recorders are made in Japan.	passive	present
We are making a doll.	active	present
The car was stolen last night.	passive	past
They were very happy.	active	past
The books were read by many people.	passive	past
Your father will be very angry.	active	future
A new hotel will be built in our street.	passive	future

 Seite 113

1. President Bush's speech was printed by a lot of newspaper editors.
2. Ailwee Cave is visited by thousands of people every summer.
3. Fred was cut in two by the magician.
4. The wedding cake had been brought in by four waiters.
5. The new Madonna CD has already been bought by more that 200,000 people.
6. Last year the World Cup was won by the French team.
7. The exhibition will be opened by the mayor next Friday.

 Seite 115

1. Dogs must be kept on the lead.
2. The patients may be visited from 4 to 7 p. m.
3. The windows couldn't be opened.
4. Raw eggs must not be heated in the microwave.
5. Fred's leg had to be bandaged.
6. The paintings must not be photographed with a flash.
7. Oysters can be eaten raw.
8. Thank God the tooth didn't have to be pulled out.

Lösungen Kapitel G

Seite 116

1. Tom was told an interesting story (by Granny).
2. Mr Smith had been sold the old Ford (by Mr Brown).
3. I was shown the way by a friendly gentleman.
4. Barbara has been sent a postcard from Australia (by one of her friends).
5. I was given a glass of orange juice by the stewardess.

Seite 117

We will be picked up at Dublin airport.
We and our baggage will be taken to a guesthouse.
We will be given special cycling maps.
Our baggage will be transported from one guesthouse to the next.
Our rooms will be booked in advance.
We will be shown where to put our bikes.
We will be told where to find inns or coffee shops on the way.

Seite 118 G13

past perfect	simple past	present perfect	simple present	future I
it had been stolen	it was stolen	it has been stolen	it is stolen	it will be stolen
he had been found	he was found	he has been found	he is found	he will be found
we had been asked	we were asked	we have been asked	we are asked	we will be asked
she had been seen	she was seen	she has been seen	she is seen	she will be seen
it had been sold	it was sold	it has been sold	it is sold	it will be sold
it had been made	it was made	it has been made	it is made	it will be made
it had been used	it was used	it has been used	it is used	it will be used
it had been written	it was written	it has been written	it is written	it will be written
they had been repaired	they were repaired	they have been repaired	they are repaired	they will be repaired

Seite 118 Test

1.
a You will be picked up at the airport by Dad.
b The car has often been repaired by Mr Brown himself.
c Tea is drunk by people all over the world.
d Mrs Barnes was offered a leading position by Skyline Enterprises.
e The soundtrack had been written by David Bowie.
f Four people and a cat had to be rescued from the burning house by the firemen.

2.
The most exciting film that has ever been made!
America is attacked by dangerous creatures.
They were sent to take away all fast food restaurants.
If they can't be stopped, New York will be destroyed!
A hero must be found who will fight against these creatures.
He has been found: Fred, the Terminator!

Kapitel H

 Seite 124

1. Barbara's brother
2. the bird's nest
3. Canada's new president
4. the boy's feet
5. men's socks
6. the pig's head
7. a one hour's break
8. children's toys
9. Germany's biggest city
10. our neighbour's dog

 Seite 125

1. the Millers' new car
2. the horses' ears
3. the twins' jackets
4. a two hours' delay
5. dogs' biscuits
6. my parents' room
7. the Greens' garden
8. a four hours' drive
9. my sisters' bikes
10. the rabbits' ears

 Seite 126

1. the name of the street/road
2. the roofs of the houses
3. the roots of the trees
4. the car of the people who/that moved in last week
5. the colour of my new umbrella
6. the names of the animals that/which live in Australia

 Seite 128

1. On Monday morning she went to the baker's and to the butcher's.
2. In the afternoon she was at the dentist's and at the chemist's.
3. She spent (the) Tuesday morning at the hairdresser's.
4. A lady asked: "Is the red sports car yours?"
   Mrs Silverstone answered: "No, it's not mine. It's my brother's."
5. From Wednesday till Saturday she stayed at her sister's.

 Seite 129

1. That's Julie, a friend of mine from Australia.
2. That's Pete. A neighbour of his is watering the flowers!
3. Charlie's uncle is a fireman. That's Charlie with some colleagues of his uncle's.
4. And that's Maggie. Juggling is a great hobby of hers.

Lösungen Kapitel H

Seite 130 H6

1. The Millers' new car has got seats for seven people.
2. The walls of my room are decorated with lots of posters.
3. A friend of mine celebrated his birthday last Saturday.
4. Linda's brother broke his leg yesterday.
5. We have a twenty minutes' break at 10.30.
6. The roof of our neighbour's house has to be repaired.
7. Is that the purse of the lady with the two poodles?
8. That's not Jane's jacket, it's Diana's./That's not Diana's jacket, it's Jane's.
9. Children's clothes are rather expensive in this shop.
10. The birds' feathers were glittering in the sun.
11. My sister had to go to the dentist's this morning.
12. The Empire State Building is one of America's highest skyscrapers.

Seite 131 Test

1. in three weeks' time
2. Her father's cousin
3. the girls' dogs
4. a photo of the house
5. The name of the girl
6. her sister's name
7. a twenty hours' flight
8. A friend of hers/One of her friends
9. At the doctor's
10. Australia's wildlife/Australia's animals

Register

f. bedeutet: Du findest das Stichwort auf der angegebenen und der folgenden Seite.
ff. bedeutet: Du findest das Stichwort auf der angegebenen und mehreren folgenden Seiten.

B
Bilder beschriften 18f.

F
Fragen und Antworten *(questions and answers)* 20ff.
   Bitten, Einladungen, Vorschläge 22ff.
   Entscheidungsfragen *(yes/no questions)* 27ff.
   Fragen mit Fragepronomen 30ff.

G
Genitiv *(genitive)* 122ff.
   doppelter Genitiv 129f.
   ohne nachfolgendes Substantiv 127f.
   of-Genitiv 126, 129ff.
   s-Genitiv 122ff., 127ff.
Gespräche führen 20ff.

H
Hören und Sprechen 57f.

I
Indirekte Rede *(reported speech)* 76ff.
   Aussagesätze 76ff.
   Befehlssätze 88ff.
   Fragesätze 84ff.
   Zeitenfolge 78ff.

K
Kurzantworten *(question tags)* 27, 29

L
Lerntechniken 18f., 37f., 57f., 74f., 94f., 104f., 120f.
Lesen *(reading)* 104f.

M
Meinungsäußerungen 32ff.

P
Passiv *(passive)* 106ff.
   Aktiv und Passiv 111ff.
   in Verbindung mit can, must und may 114f.
   persönliches Passiv 116f.
   Zeitformen 107ff., 118

R
Rechtschreibung *(spelling)* 120f.

S
Sprechen *(talking)* 20ff., 74f.

T
Telefonieren *(telephoning)* 25f.

U
Unbestimmte Pronomen 96ff.
   each – every 99f.
   (a) little – (a) few 101f.
   much – many – a lot (of) 100f.
   some – any 96ff.
Unregelmäßige Verben *(irregular verbs)* 10ff.
Unvollständige Hilfsverben *(defective auxiliaries)* 59ff., 70ff.
   can und Ersatzformen 59ff., 70f.
   may und Ersatzformen 62f., 70f.
   must und Ersatzformen 64ff., 70f.

V
Verlaufsform *(progressive form)* 39f., 48f., 53f.

W

Wörterbuch *(dictionary)* 37f., 94f.
Wörter lernen 18f., 120f.

Z

Zeiten *(tenses)* 7ff., 39ff.
  Bildung der Zeiten 7ff.
  present perfect mit since und for 50ff.
  simple past und *past progressive* 48f.
  simple past und *present perfect* 40ff.

Null Bock auf schlechte Noten?

... dann nimm doch mentor!

- **mentor Lektüre Durchblick**
  Inhalt, Hintergrund und Interpretation für Deutsch- und Englisch-Lektüren ab Klasse 9/10

- **mentor Grundwissen**
  Umfassende Darstellung der Themen eines Fachs bis zur 10. Klasse
  (Fächer: Deutsch, Englisch, Spanisch, Geschichte, Geografie, Mathematik, Biologie, Chemie, Physik)

- **mentor Audio-Lernhilfen**
  Leichter lernen mit Rap und Hip-Hop:
  Hear them, rap them, know them!

- **Lernen leicht gemacht**
  Clevere Tipps für mehr Erfolg in allen Fächern – speziell für die einzelnen Altersstufen

Infos, Lerntipps & mehr
www.mentor.de

mentor
Eine Klasse besser.

Büffel(n) ist out!

mentor liefert das Wissen, das dir noch fehlt

- **mentor Lern- und Abiturhilfen**
  Selbsthilfe statt Nachhilfe für alle wichtigen Fächer von der
  3. Klasse bis zum Abitur
  *(Fächer: Deutsch, Englisch, Französisch, Latein,
  Mathematik, Biologie, Chemie, Physik)*

- **mentor training XXL**
  Regeln – Übungen – Lösungen
  Die wichtigsten Themen der Fächer Deutsch, Englisch und Mathematik
  jeweils in einem Band. Für die Klassen 5 – 10

- **Lernen leicht gemacht**
  Clevere Tipps für mehr Erfolg in allen Fächern –
  speziell für die einzelnen Altersstufen

Infos, Lerntipps & mehr
www.mentor.de

mentor
Eine Klasse besser.